THE BATTLE OF LINCOLN PARK

THE BATTLE OF LINCOLN PARK

Urban Renewal and Gentrification in Chicago

Daniel Kay Hertz

Belt Publishing

Printed in the United States of America
First edition 2018

ISBN: 978-1-94874-209-2

Belt Publishing
2306 West 17th Street, Suite 4
Cleveland, Ohio 44113
www.beltpublishing.com

Book design by Meredith Pangrace
Cover by David Wilson

CONTENTS:

1,000 ft.

Chicago's North Side, Early to Mid 20th Century

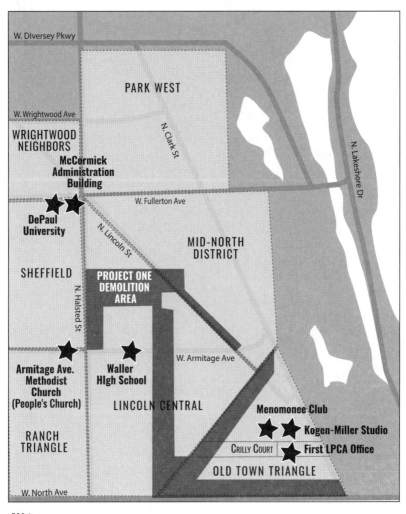

**Neighborhood Associations Affiliated with the
Lincoln Park Conservation Association**

INTRODUCTION

In December 1969, Stephen Shamberg resigned as president of one of the most powerful neighborhood organizations in Chicago, the Lincoln Park Conservation Association. In his letter of resignation, he offered a blunt assessment of the movement.

"We are assisting," he wrote, "in the destruction of our community."

For fifteen years, LPCA had fought to transform its piece of the city's North Side, just two miles from downtown on the shores of Lake Michigan. And indeed, Lincoln Park had been transformed. Dilapidated homes boasted new windows and paint; developers clamored to invest where banks had refused to lend; and new businesses were opening. But not all of its members were feeling triumphant. Instead, they found themselves bitterly divided: Some feared their decades of work might soon be rolled back. Others believed it deserved to be.

Back in the 1940s, when the antique dealers, historians, and lawyers were just beginning their campaign to restore Lincoln Park's Victorian-era grandeur, they had felt no such ambiguity. Back then, the stakes had seemed very different to them, their campaign to remake the neighborhood almost utopian.

In the years after World War II, Lincoln Park was an aging neighborhood of walkup apartments, the lake on one side and an industrial riverfront on the other. Close to downtown Chicago, and even closer to the elite Gold Coast area, its residents' incomes nevertheless ranked sixtieth out of the city's seventy-five neighborhoods. Despite a notable lack of racial integration—more than ninety-eight percent of Lincoln Parkers were white—almost the entire neighborhood was "redlined," or cut off from home loans for purchases or renovations, a type of disinvestment often targeted at black communities. Home to more than 100,000 people, busy commercial streetscapes, and longstanding religious and ethnic communities, most members of the white middle class nevertheless believed it was a neighborhood without a future. For them, Lincoln Park was destined for further economic decline, perhaps even racial integration from the small black community to the south—and, if things could not be turned around, annihilation through government-led "slum clearance."

At the same time, a small but growing movement of white professionals viewed Lincoln Park as a gem waiting to be polished and reclaimed. In the late 1800s, families of means had built stately brick homes and apartments on the rubble of the Great Fire of 1871, before ultimately abandoning them in the march towards the suburbs. Now postwar "rehabbers"—generally professional-class white homeowners who bought and renovated old homes—cited that history as proof Lincoln Park deserved a more illustrious future. If they fixed up the old homes and modernized nearby streets and storefronts, they insisted, Lincoln Park might enjoy every advantage of a new suburban subdivision—with all the history, culture, and convenience of the city. Its future might not be decline and demolition, but rebirth as a new kind of community that combined the best of both worlds.

But things had changed by 1969. People no longer wondered whether middle-class white people might settle down in an old urban neighborhood like Lincoln Park: It had already happened, and much of the eastern side of the community was now well above citywide averages in income and education. The new question seemed to be whether they could leave room for anyone else. As incomes rose, so did rents; each home renovation— increasingly performed by professional investors as much as individual families—increased property values. Meanwhile, the urban renewal program LPCA had lobbied for had demolished entire streetscapes, displacing thousands of people who were disproportionately low-income, Latino, or black.

Many now wondered if the future of Lincoln Park was the social homogeneity of the suburbs transplanted to the urban core. Shamberg was not alone in questioning whether the movement he led might be ruining the neighborhood it had meant to save.

The Battle of Lincoln Park traces the rehabbers' path from idealism in the 1940s and 1950s to existential crisis in the late 1960s and early 1970s, and Lincoln Park's path from a predominantly working class neighborhood to one of the wealthiest communities in the Chicago area. The rest of the book is divided into three parts. Part One, "The Invention of Old Town," follows the earliest bohemian rehabbers on the North Side and their more middle-class successors who laid the groundwork to bring urban renewal to Lincoln Park.

Part Two, "The Conservation of Lincoln Park," covers the period when the rehabbers aggressively pursued their own private neighborhood improvement program as federal officials dragged their feet.

Part Three, "The Battle of Lincoln Park," tells the story of the rising resistance that emerged after the start of the federal renewal program and fought for its own visions of the neighborhood, and the uneasy resolution of that conflict.

Along the way, this book will try to show how the rehabbers' work interacted with larger social and economic systems to create Lincoln Park as it exists today: the heart of a predominantly white zone of concentrated affluence that encompasses more than half a million people over a large part of Chicago's North Side. Just as the twentieth century history of redlining, white flight, and racist violence helps us understand why cities like Chicago have large, disproportionately black and Latino areas of disinvestment, the twentieth century history of slumming, conservation movements, and rehabbing helps explain why we have large, predominantly white, areas of concentrated investment.

Much of Lincoln Park's path in the years after World War Two will seem familiar to people who live in gentrifying neighborhoods now—from the way that new middle-class residents praised the neighborhood's authenticity and diversity, to complaints about commercialization, to the organizing taken up by lower-income residents and their allies to preserve their place in the neighborhood. (By "gentrifying," I mean a growth in professional class residents, generally without social ties to the prior residents of the neighborhood, and usually white.) If we recognize ourselves and our neighborhoods today in the earlier experiences of Lincoln Park, we may have a better sense of where we are going, and why.

The Battle of Lincoln Park also makes several arguments about gentrification in Chicago.

First, it argues that gentrification is a much older process than we often assume, with roots stretching back nearly to the beginning of the twentieth century. Short memories about the trend of increasing affluence on the North Side seem to be almost as old: Between the 1930s and 1960s, Chicago media published articles every few years claiming to have discovered a "rebirth" in Lincoln Park, few of which acknowledged earlier versions of the same story. Many of these articles are remarkably similar to those published today about the communities currently undergoing similar changes.

This long history is not just a curiosity. The consistent growth of a relatively affluent, predominantly white area on the North Side for more than seventy-five years challenges many of the most commonly offered explanations for gentrification today. These explanations—which hinge on new developments like a post-recession economy or the consumer preferences of the millennial generation—may very well shape the path of neighborhood change. But if the underlying trend predates them by the better part of a century, they cannot be the whole story.

Second, growing wealth in parts of central Chicago cannot be separated from growing disinvestment in other neighborhoods. These opposite paths are not contradictions, or a "tale of two cities." Lincoln Park's evolution into an affluent community does not make sense except in the context of the growing poverty—and growing black and Latino population—in much of the rest of Chicago. White middle-class residents responded to the threat of economic decline and loss of racial majority status by concentrating their investments in a tightly drawn, slowly expanding circle centered on already-established strongholds of the upper middle class. It was this concentration that both bid up housing prices and segregated professional whites within the circle, while withdrawing investments from areas outside it.

This also means that disinvestment and hyperinvestment, suburban flight and gentrification have all been happening simultaneously since the early twentieth century. The simpler story—that Chicago, like many other American cities, had a distinct period of economic decline as whites fled for the suburbs after World War II and then a distinct period of resurgence as young people returned to the city in the 1990s and afterwards—covers up a much more complicated reality. Lincoln Parkers created a template for the white middle class revival of urban neighborhoods even as suburbanization reached a fever pitch. In fact, between 1950 and 1970, both trends existed within Lincoln Park itself, with much of its western side becoming deeply disinvested while its eastern side became significantly wealthier.

Third, neighborhood change in Lincoln Park was not mainly the result of individuals' actions, but of economic, political, and social systems. Many people worked very hard to make Lincoln Park a predominantly white, middle-class community—but so did many others in neighborhoods across the city. Most of them failed. The rehabbers in Lincoln Park were successful not because of their special ingenuity, but because of their position in interlocking social, political, and economic systems, such as ongoing efforts to segregate black Chicagoans on the South and West Sides, and the combination of happenstance and public policy that created a permanent stronghold of the wealthy in the Gold Coast just south of Lincoln Park in the early twentieth century.

Finally, this story shows how neighborhood change leads residents to compete over who has the authority to speak for and define their community—but also the limits of that authority. Many Lincoln Parkers who did not belong to the rehabbing movement, of course, did not feel that their neighborhood needed "saving" by relative newcomers. These residents, who tended to have lived in the area longer, have lower incomes, or both, argued they had the right to speak for the neighborhood because of their deeper roots in the area or greater numbers.

The middle class homeowners who organized to "conserve" Lincoln Park justified their role as stewards of the neighborhood with a different narrative. In their telling, they were the only people with the vision, skills, and resources to triumphantly restore Lincoln Park's authentic identity—its Victorian-era status as a predominantly middle-class community. This narrative played a powerful role in the first decades of the rehabbing movement, giving relative newcomers to the area a sense of confidence and unity of purpose in reshaping the neighborhood.

Their confidence was eventually broken, however, by sustained organizing on the part of residents who opposed the rehabbers' changes. These challenges split the rehabbers in two, as even some former leaders came to believe that the moral authority to chart the future of Lincoln Park belonged to their opponents.

And yet even with such public defections, those who wanted to put the brakes on Lincoln Park's evolution into an exclusive, high-income community found it difficult to do so. Moral authority was not a substitute for economic, social, or political power. As government-led demolitions and private renovations evicted thousands from the neighborhood—and some rehabbers increasingly viewed their opposition as a threat to the new Lincoln Park they had built—the battle became more desperate. Petitions and counter-petitions gave way to smashed windows, bombings, and death threats. Out of this battle, modern Lincoln Park was born.

PART ONE

THE INVENTION OF OLD TOWN
1917-1956

CHAPTER 1
TOWER TOWN AND THE GOLD COAST

A few months before the end of World War I, two teenagers staged an art school rebellion in Chicago. Sol Kogen and Edgar Miller came from very different places—Kogen, Chicago-born to Russian Jewish immigrants; Miller, a small-town boy from Idaho—but they were both seventeen, and they both chafed at the expectations of their instructors at the prestigious Art Institute.

Calling themselves "the Independents," they quit the Institute—or, in some tellings, they were expelled. In any case, Kogen and Miller began the year 1917 as students on the grand downtown boulevard of Michigan Avenue, and ended it just a few miles away, at Jane Addams's Hull House, a settlement house in a rundown immigrant neighborhood on the West Side.

They thrived at Hull House. For Kogen, it was a return to his roots, just a few blocks from the women's accessory shop his father owned on busy Maxwell Street. Miller, who had been hired at age eleven to do watercolor renderings for a local architecture firm, honed his skills as an artistic polymath, producing everything from woodwork and metal sculpting to oil painting and stained glass.

Then, for a period, their paths diverged. Kogen inherited his father's business and ran it with unlikely success, growing from a single storefront on Maxwell Street to a small empire with four locations, including one in the downtown Loop. By twenty-five, he was rich, and could afford to become a bohemian. He sold his share of the business and moved to Paris to study art.

Edgar Miller became a successful commercial artist. He made advertising posters for Marshall Field's department store, then began an apprenticeship with a prominent architectural sculptor and received commissions at Northwestern University, the North Dakota state capitol, and executive offices in downtown skyscrapers. Just four years after the Independents stormed out of the School of the Art Institute, Miller returned as an instructor.

When Kogen returned from Paris in 1926, his head was full of ideas from his time in the neighborhood of Montmartre, where artists had moved into studios to experiment with new ways of living and creating together. In 1927, he bought an old apartment building at 155 Carl Street in what a national magazine would later call "the heart of the near north side slums." He quickly bought another building on Wells Street just a few blocks north, and hired his old friend Miller to transform both into artists' studios. Miller, in turn, brought on Jesus Torres, an immigrant from Mexico who had spent years working in cotton fields and stockyards before others recognized his artistic talent at Hull House.

Together, they deconstructed the three-story brick flats, rebuilding the walls with architectural scraps, laying out intimate courtyards, and turning doorways into soaring atria. From the mosaic ceilings to the woodworked staircases to the stained glass windows, no surface was less than exuberant. In Miller's words, they had taken an "obsolete" building and created "something new, fascinating, and living."

The special care and creativity that Miller and Torres put into their work also meant that the studios they created almost immediately rented for more than what any but the most commercially successful artists could afford. Other factors also pushed higher-paying renters to what became known as the Carl Street colony. A boom in lakefront apartment construction had come to a sudden end with the start of the Great Depression in 1929; without a steady stream of new apartments, would-be renters were forced to look to older, renovated housing, creating a line of potential takers for Kogen's studios. As each unit was completed and rented, the team secured a stream of income with which to renovate the next one.

Meanwhile, Kogen's artistical and financial success inspired copycats looking to join a community of creative renovators on Carl Street. Buying and rehabilitating a building—even a cheap one—required more resources than were available to a typical artist. But Carl Street did tend to attract people with a certain sensibility. A retired baritone with the Metropolitan Opera bought an old rooming house to renovate; then a professor at the School of the Art Institute. They were joined by an army captain and his wife, who fancied themselves amateur photographers. A pair of commercial artists bought up three buildings in a row directly across from Kogen's building.

These rehabbers believed they were doing more than working on their own home improvement projects. For them, Carl Street was an opportunity to build a new community of creative, freethinking people. They hosted an annual art fair, and celebrated Halloween and New Year's together. At the neighborhood Christmas party, someone would dig a pit in their backyard, light a fire, and roast a pig amid the snow.

The street this clique sought to remake according to their own dreams was neither a blank slate nor a timeless community preserved in amber. Kogen and his followers were just the latest in a long history of sweeping changes. A century before, the area had been a prairie between the lake and a small Potawatomi village; it had then been settled as cabbage farms by German immigrants in the 1830s, built up with small, tightly packed cottages in the

1850s, and burned to the ground in the Great Chicago Fire of 1871. After the Fire, it was rebuilt first with brick houses and then, as the city's population exploded at the end of the 1800s, with three and four story apartment flats. For a few decades after the Fire it had been a popular neighborhood for the upwardly mobile middle class, particularly among German immigrants and their children, but as the city continued to grow they moved on to newer neighborhoods farther from downtown. Many of the homeowners who remained earned extra income by subletting rooms to boarders looking for cheap housing close to factories and downtown service work. By 1920, there were twenty-five boarders living in the dozen or so buildings fronting Carl Street, in addition to the more formal tenants and homeowners. Though nearly all of the area's residents were white, many were immigrants from Germany or elsewhere in Europe. When a rehabber bought a property to convert, often the first step was to evict these boarders and tenants, who would then need to find housing elsewhere in the area.

In 1942, a *Tribune* reporter came to profile the block. She found "one big happy family": "artists and their friends," as well as "businessmen...seeking to live...near the nightlife of the Near North Side, with the taste of an exotic and Bohemian lifestyle."

By then, all but four buildings on the street had been bought up, remodeled, and added to the colony. At the time, the little Midwestern Montmartre was surrounded by run-down rooming houses and two-family cottages. In a few decades, it would be one of the richest inner city neighborhoods in America.

———————————

The Carl and Wells street colonies were a harbinger of neighborhood change to come. They were also the product of neighborhood change that had already taken place. To understand why Kogen settled on the Near North Side—and not, for example, the area near his native Maxwell Street on the West Side—you have to go back to two other Chicago communities: Tower Town and the Gold Coast.

In many ways, Kogen, Miller, and Torres were building on the model of Tower Town as much as on that of Paris. Tower Town, too, had grown up around a community of artists' studios, but of a more genteel kind. Back in 1894, a judge and art patron named Lambert Tree built a studio complex at Ohio and State Streets, one and a half miles south of Carl, in the middle of what was then a wealthy mansion district. The Tree Studio Building provided a wholesome environment at an affordable price so artists could live comfortably in the central city.

Soon, however, the wealthy began to leave the area around the Tree Studio Building. They felt their exclusive enclave was threatened by Chicago's booming downtown, which brought new businesses—and their working-class employees—even closer to the mansions. As aristocratic families left, their large homes were often subdivided into cheap apartments.

By the 1910s, rents had fallen far enough that artists did not need a judge's subsidy to live in the area. They could make their own studios out of the run-down buildings, and they did. The result, for a time, was a cultural community that built a national reputation. It came to be called Tower Town, after the landmark water tower that survived the Fire of 1871.

Artistic and literary celebrities lived in Tower Town, including the novelist Sherwood Anderson, the poet Carl Sandburg, and Harriet Monroe, the founder of *Poetry* magazine. But its real cachet came from the thousands of people from around the country who arrived to debate ideas, experience things, and live in ways that would be unacceptable almost anywhere else. The epitome of the Tower Town ethos was the Dill Pickle Club—a cabaret, social club, and lecture hall founded by a socialist named Jack Jones in 1917. Built to accommodate the growing crowds at the weekly talks he was holding at a radical bookstore nearby, it quickly became a neighborhood hub. The Dill Pickle hosted forums on radical political and social ideas, attracting, in the words of one regular, "pale girls with daring bobbed heads…and tortoise-shell glasses discuss[ing] Nietzsche…with boys whose eyes dreamed and visioned."

Tower Town offered other kinds of provocations, too. Some, like the frankly sexual cabaret performances, visitors could simply observe. Others invited full participation. On St. Patrick's Day and Halloween, the Dill Pickle threw masquerade balls in which women and men competed for the title of "Best Adam and Eve Costume."

This sexual freedom was as important to Tower Town's identity as its creative or political ferment. Residents found a place where living with your unmarried partner was not just acceptable, but common, and where one could take up romantic relationships on a whim: "Because you like the back of someone's head," one Tower Towner explained, "or agree that…the proletariat is being crushed under capital's heel." Visitors—including a number of students who traveled from the relatively distant Northwestern University or the University of Chicago—might find a partner for a single night of experimentation before returning to their well-chaperoned campus.

"There's at least a year in everybody's life when he wants to do as he pleases," one young man told Harvey Zorbaugh, a sociologist whose book *The Gold Coast and the Slum* investigated the neighborhood. Tower Town "is the only place where he can do it without sneaking off in a hole by himself."

For many, however, it was about more than a year or two of rebellion. The Dill Pickle Club, along with other Tower Town hangouts, was also a center of gay and lesbian social life. Some venues put on drag shows; in many, same-sex displays of affection went uncommented on, except by those unfamiliar with the neighborhood.

A nearby beachfront area was known as a gathering place for gay men in good weather.

Tower Town did retain at least one kind of social barrier, however: throughout this period, almost all of its residents were white. While it existed firmly outside of polite middle-class white society, it kept itself socially distinct from the most impoverished areas to its west, where a rapidly growing black community and an older Sicilian one butted up against the industrial riverfront. That neighborhood, known in the city's newspapers as "Little Hell," would remain among Chicago's poorest for the rest of the twentieth century, in no small part because of racism. Tower Town, on the other hand, would soon see money again.

In fact, Tower Town had never quite been out of sight of money to begin with. The neighborhood was attractive to artists in part because the rich had abandoned their mansions, allowing students and painters to rent a room in them at reasonable prices. But it was also attractive because the rich—on whom many artists relied for jobs or patronage—had not gone too far. It was attractive, in other words, because of the Gold Coast.

A narrow, three-block-wide strip of land tucked along Lake Shore Drive, the Gold Coast was the last stronghold of the upper class in Chicago's early twentieth century urban core. Its elite families had fled from at least three older, defunct concentrations of privilege: one on the South Side around Prairie Avenue; one on the West Side on Ashland Boulevard; and the old Near North district that had become Tower Town.

The founder of the Gold Coast was the real estate magnate Potter Palmer, who abandoned his Prairie Avenue mansion to build a 10,000-square-foot castle on Lake Shore Drive in 1882. Many others followed in the 1890s. They fled the south lakefront, which was crowded with railroads, and the Near West Side, with its rapidly expanding lower-class immigrant district, for the picturesque North Lake Shore Drive. The Drive was close to downtown but relatively isolated: Pine Street, a major thoroughfare, lacked a bridge over the Chicago River to the Loop, and the nearest streetcar lines—which attracted shops and crowds wherever they went—were a safe distance to the west.

By the 1910s, the Gold Coast was home to the city's most prominent business, civic, and high society personalities. Its residents owned Loop real estate and sponsored elite cultural institutions. And their money—plus that of the middle-class residents of other neighborhoods in the Gold Coast's social orbit—helped support Tower Town.

Some of this support was direct, as with the Tree Studio Building or the Three Arts Club, which was established nearby in 1912 to provide low-cost apartments for young women artists. Some of it was indirect, as with the downtown art schools, theaters, and movie palaces where many Tower Town residents either studied or worked. And some of it was more discreet. College students weren't the only people to visit the neighborhood for sex tourism: Many young artists found that they could support themselves by finding a wealthy patron looking for up close exposure to cultural ferment and, sometimes, more. "Any tenth-rate free-verse poet," one Tower Towner reported, "could find a capable and efficient stenographer to type his manuscripts, buy his clothes, pay his rent, and sleep with him."

Tower Towners depended on the wealth that radiated from the Gold Coast, and so they were also at its mercy. The freewheeling, out-of-sight atmosphere that made bohemia attractive to begin with was only possible because of its distance from the high rents and social judgment of "polite society." But that distance was never as great as it seemed, and was constantly shrinking under the pressure to commercialize the neighborhood.

This pressure became even greater with the passage of Prohibition in 1920. Suddenly, the distinction between licit and illicit nightlife was gone: Any place that would offer you a drink was operating beyond the reach of the law. These blurred lines encouraged a "slumming" craze that would last through the next decade.

Slummers were members of the middle or upper class looking for a thrill by patronizing entertainment venues either in low-income white or black neighborhoods. And places like Tower Town—whose "slum" environs were made more approachable by the presence of artists—were among the most popular destinations.

Also in 1920, construction crews completed the Michigan Avenue bridge, which linked the elite Loop boulevard with Pine Street north of the river. Like elevated highways half a century later, the heavily-trafficked river had been a formidable barrier, and had historically kept the city's downtown business district from expanding too rapidly on the near north side. But the Michigan Avenue bridge struck down that barrier. Pine was renamed North Michigan, and its townhomes began to give way to the shops and businesses that characterized Michigan Avenue south of the river.

Many Tower Towners weren't opposed to commercialization; some actively invited it. The managers of the Dill Pickle, realizing that high-paying customers were looking for an atmosphere of titillating danger, supposedly had the club raided by the police a few times, earning it a note in the papers, and started to charge admission. Nearby, a group of young women offered a "Seeing Bohemia" tour and took wide-eyed tourists through local studios— decorated extravagantly to be sure there would be something to see—in exchange for seventy-five cents a head.

But the very presence of these new slummers and their money changed the neighborhood. New bars and cabarets, facsimiles of the "authentic" Tower Town experience, popped up specifically to serve them. Older establishments strategized about how to attract their business. Even as longtime Tower Towners

27

remade their community to profit from them, they felt the slummers were ruining it. Jack Jones, the owner of the Dill Pickle, complained about their boorish behavior. The artists at the Tree Studio Building called the police to break up late-night crowds outside the slummer-friendly Classic Cafe across the street.

Most of all, people who wanted only to be tourists, rather than artists, made the true believers in Tower Town feel that the community no longer belonged to them. The neighborhood's reputation shifted from that of a true bohemia to one full of "poseurs," "dilettantes," and "hangers-on." Adding injury to insult, some slummers began not just to visit but to live in the neighborhood, contributing to the pressure on rents from the expansion of downtown. By the late twenties, it was no longer possible for a starving artist to afford Tower Town apartments, and many of the old rundown mansions were replaced by office buildings and high-end hotels.

And yet, for all the reasons that had brought them near the Gold Coast to begin with, many of the bohemians who left the area would not escape its orbit. While some fled to cities like New York, others looking for what Tower Town had been simply put their bags down on the next block up the lakefront where the price was right. For Sol Kogen, that was Carl Street.

––––––––––––––––

The rise and fall of Tower Town and the rise of what would become Old Town marked a pattern that would repeat time and time again over the coming generations. People on the social fringes of affluent Chicago set up communities on the physical fringes of affluent neighborhoods, close enough to make a living from their wealth but far enough to avoid high rents and disapproving looks. But the communities they helped to build were attractive to many more firmly middle-class or upper-middle-class Chicagoans, for cultural reasons (the draw of a bohemian lifestyle) and structural ones (the allure of short commutes to both art schools and insurance firms).

In some important ways, however, the Kogen-Miller-Torres studios on Carl and Wells streets would start a new pattern, unlike the one Tower Town had followed. A hint of that new pattern was evident in the fate of the Gold Coast.

By the end of the 1920s, it seemed obvious to people like sociologist Harvey Zorbaugh that the Gold Coast's days were numbered. Chicago's older upper-class districts had all perished, and each in the same way: an invasion of commercial and industrial firms looking for new land on which to expand the central business district, and the dense lower-class apartments that sprung up to house their workers. Similar decline had struck over and over in other cities as well; in Manhattan, elites had steadily moved uptown over the course of the 19th century to escape development spreading from the bottom of the island. In the face of this process, few aristocratic communities had lasted for more than a generation, and the Gold Coast was unlikely to be very different.

But Zorbaugh was wrong. Far from passing away, the Gold Coast has remained one of Chicago's most exclusive neighborhoods for over a century, and shows little sign of flagging as of the late 2010s.

What was the difference between the Gold Coast and Ashland Boulevard or Prairie Avenue? Gold Coast residents at the time credited a new legal tool for preserving their neighborhood's exclusivity: zoning.

In the early 1920s, North Michigan Avenue was rapidly commercializing, and businesses threatened to colonize an elite stretch of homes on nearby Lake Shore Drive in the Gold Coast. Locals feared that if businesses were allowed to open, "the residential desirability of the Drive would [be] destroyed," and the whole neighborhood would be abandoned by the rich—just like Prairie Avenue, Ashland Boulevard, and the area that became Tower Town.

At the same time, the City Council was drafting Chicago's first zoning code. Pioneered just a few years earlier by wealthy Manhattan merchants, zoning laws allowed cities to require a particular use—homes, business, industry, and so on—for every parcel of land. As in Manhattan, proponents in Chicago stressed that these codes could preserve high property values in districts like the Gold Coast and end the elite neighborhoods' cycle of boom and bust. The state law giving cities in Illinois the legal right to zone cited a housing expert who warned that without regulation, "a process of deterioration sets in to [wealthy neighborhoods]...: Large houses fall into working-class hands, and are let and sub-let, and the street loses caste." Zoning would "save" neighborhoods like the Gold Coast from this fate.

Critics of zoning agreed that it would likely preserve such aristocratic districts, but disagreed about whether this was a good thing. A federal judge actually struck down zoning codes as unconstitutional in 1924. "In the last analysis," the judge wrote, "the result...is to classify the population and segregate them according to their income." But a few years later, the U.S. Supreme Court reversed that decision and upheld zoning.

In the Gold Coast, wealthy residents squared off against business leaders to lobby the City Council over the zoning of Lake Shore Drive. Ultimately, the residents carried the day, and the Council banned commercial activity. Gold Coasters were satisfied that "the nature of the neighborhood [would] not be materially changed." And so it wasn't: Though zoning is surely not the only reason, the Gold Coast has remained an economically (and for the most part, racially) segregated enclave ever since.

The Gold Coast's staying power as an elite enclave set the stage for the transformation of Old Town, Lincoln Park, and a growing section of the North Side over the rest of the 20th century.

First, if the Gold Coast had fallen into disrepair like the earlier aristocratic communities, the anchor that held people like Kogen, Miller, and Torres—and those who would join them later—to the near North Side would have been much weaker. Those who needed to live on the fringes of affluent society would have had to chase those fringes around the city as Chicago's elites jumped from one neighborhood to the next.

Instead, with the core of the downtown rich locked in place, the fringes began simply to move outward as more and more people arrived to participate in middle-class urban life. Rather than trailing behind a mobile elite constantly outrunning the city's commerce and commercial workers, they began to create a stable and growing zone of affluence that gradually incorporated more and more of the North Side.

The legal tool of zoning also explains a great deal of why the neighborhood change that followed the Kogen-Miller colony looked so different, in many ways, from that which claimed Tower Town.

In Tower Town, as land values increased, bohemians were chased out by higher-density, more commercial land uses: Offices, hotels, and highrise apartments intended for middle-class workers. But their successors to the north would aggressively use zoning to fend off these invaders. So while developers successfully built a strip of taller buildings along the lakefront, and a booming Wells Street shopping district became a weekend carnival of bars and cafes, the vast majority of Lincoln Park would be spared such transformations. In fact, the neighborhood's most dramatic changes occurred alongside a dramatic *fall* in density. These declines meant that the same number of middle-class arrivals would be spread over a larger area, affecting a greater number of communities.

CHAPTER 2
REHABBING AND REDLINING

J ust a few blocks north of the Kogen-Miller-Torres colony on
Carl Street and around the corner from Kogen's Wells Street
studios, another block was undergoing a similar transformation
in the 1930s.

Crilly Court had been built by a developer named Daniel Crilly
after the Fire of 1871. Crilly cut the block-long street through a property
he owned in an attractive area just west of the lakefront park, building
twelve row houses on one side and an apartment flat on the other.

Like the rest of the neighborhood, Crilly Court began as a
solidly middle class address and began to travel down the economic
ladder—and out of sight of middle class society—after the turn of
the century. In 1924, a World War I veteran named Henry Gerber
made his Crilly Court apartment the headquarters of the Society
for Human Rights, the first gay rights organization in the United
States, and its newspaper, *Friendship and Freedom*. This turned out
to be too extreme even for a block that boasted a brothel at either
end of the street; the next year Gerber's home was raided by the
police, and he fled to New York.

But just like on Carl Street, the slowdown in new high-end
apartments during the Depression brought an increasing number

of middle class people to Crilly Court looking for suitable homes to renovate close to downtown. At first, these tended to be young adults who had grown up in tony North Shore suburbs and who left Crilly Court as they married. But Edgar Crilly, who had taken over management of the street's rental properties from his father, took advantage of the renewed interest to do his own renovations in exchange for higher rents.

As on Carl Street, these renovations meant the elimination of housing that had been priced for lower-income tenants. But for a while, it seemed that the street's working class identity and its new, more upwardly mobile identity could coexist. In 1940, one townhome housed an old, German-born couple, renting rooms to five lodgers, including a bricklayer and a porter, none of whom had more than an eighth grade education. A few doors down, a college-educated banker and his wife lived alone with their baby. Across the street in the apartment building, journalists, artists, and secretaries lived in adjoining units. And nearly all of the surrounding streets remained low-rent.

By that time, some of Crilly Court's newer residents were making regular appearances in Chicago's society pages, something that would have seemed impossible only a decade before. Despite the remaining working class tenants, the street had firmly established itself in the Gold Coast's social orbit—and at least some people, like Edgar Crilly, believed it could be brought much closer.

———

Not everyone saw affluence in the future of Crilly Court and Carl Street, though. In 1940, federal inspectors arrived from Washington and declared that the whole neighborhood was in terminal decline.

The inspectors worked for a New Deal agency called the Home Owners' Loan Corporation (HOLC), which aimed to stabilize the country's housing market—still shaky from the Depression—by purchasing home mortgages from banks. But HOLC only wanted to buy mortgages in neighborhoods with stable or growing property values. To avoid making "bad" purchases, it dispatched workers across the country to grade neighborhoods on a four-letter scale, from A ("Best") to D ("Hazardous"). The worst areas, marked in red on official maps, would be ineligible for federal support. Later, this practice would be called "redlining," and would be linked to decades of disinvestment.

Both Carl Street and Crilly Court were redlined.

"Area is badly cut up," the report on the Crilly Court area concluded. "Rooming house use…now predominates. Properties are obsolete, of poor appearance." The neighborhood had some advantages, HOLC allowed: the lake, convenient transportation to downtown jobs and shopping. "But the class of structures… limits appeal to lower class occupancy. Future appears to be one of continuing decline."

Why did HOLC see a condemned neighborhood where others like the *Tribune* and Edgar Crilly saw a template for revitalization? For a wide variety of reasons, HOLC fundamentally believed that older urban areas were incompatible with modern middle-class life. And it had compelling evidence: Middle-class whites had been moving farther and farther from city centers for decades.

Ever since the mid-1800s, when new urban railroads made it possible to travel miles to and from work, people who could afford the fares had increasingly commuted from bedroom communities far from downtowns. This suburbanization picked up markedly in the first half of the 1900s, as new transportation technologies, from streetcars to subways, allowed people to live further and further from the old urban cores. Meanwhile, a growing cultural movement—heavily promoted by real estate interests and the federal government—worked to convince Americans that single family houses, rather than apartments, were the only proper homes for families.

And then there were the cars. In 1905, there were more than a thousand Americans for every registered automobile. In 1920, it was thirteen; in 1930, five. On the eve of the Depression, in places like Milwaukee and Kansas City, already more than half of downtown commuters drove to work. There, and even more so in much denser cities like Chicago, it was becoming clear that roads designed for pedestrians and streetcars simply didn't have the capacity to handle the coming car traffic. Driving became another reason to move out to the more spacious suburbs, where roads were less clogged and parking less of a challenge. Or, as Henry Ford put it: "The city is doomed."

All these forces buffeted Chicago's inner neighborhoods. Though the city as a whole grew by well over a million people between 1910 and 1934, virtually all of that growth came in neighborhoods at least several miles from downtown. The city's older center—the rings of development that included Crilly Court and Carl Street—lost hundreds of thousands of people.

This exodus of mostly middle-class and wealthy American-born whites exacerbated the economic challenges of the central cities. Older, denser neighborhoods were abandoned to marginalized groups like the poor, immigrants, and African Americans. These groups inherited the oldest housing and infrastructure in their regions, but often lacked the financial ability to maintain or improve it.

Beyond technological and cultural trends, race played a fundamental role in the stigmatization of the inner city. Simply put, middle-class whites' avoidance of older, denser neighborhoods paled in comparison to the panic and violence that surrounded the arrival of black people.

This had not always been the case. At the start of the first Great Migration of Southern African-Americans in the early 1900s, Chicago had been a nearly all-white city, but one whose small black community was not necessarily more segregated than white ethnic groups like Italians.

But as the city's black population grew—from about 40,000 in 1910 to nearly 280,000 in 1940—whites undertook a multi-pronged campaign to ghettoize these new Chicagoans. Property owners wrote legal covenants that prohibited future owners from selling to black people; neighbors and tenants openly pressured landlords not to rent to them. Where these efforts failed, many white people were ready to enforce segregation with violence. Blacks quickly realized that violating the color line meant risking their property and their lives. From 1917 to 1921, a black home was bombed on average every twenty days; in 1919, a black boy swimming at a South Side beach whites had claimed off limits to blacks was killed by a group of white children, setting off nearly a week of organized violence that left twenty-three blacks and fifteen whites dead and more than 500 people injured.

This combination of legal tools, formal and informal persuasion, and violence proved effective. As late as 1920, not a single Census tract in Chicago was over ninety percent black; by 1930, two out of every three black Chicagoans lived in such a neighborhood, and by 1940, three out of four did. The vast majority of these neighborhoods were located in a thin strip running south from the Loop, sometimes called the "Black Belt" or Bronzeville. A smaller number were scattered around the West, far South, and near North Sides—the latter just a short walk to Carl and Wells Streets.

Neighborhoods that whites abandoned and blacks moved into usually saw their real estate prices *increase*, and often drastically: the very fact that black Chicagoans had so few safe housing options meant that landlords could charge prices that whites would never have been willing to pay. But this exploitation, along with discrimination in the provision of city services and by private businesses, also meant that these neighborhoods' physical environments often deteriorated rapidly. Landlords chose not to maintain their buildings, and often modified them in ways that boosted profits but created serious fire and safety hazards; public streets and parks were left to decay.

The federal government, through HOLC and other policies, endorsed these racist outcomes. In addition to noting the physical characteristics of the neighborhoods they inspected, HOLC's surveys included a line to note the racial status of residents, and whether that status was changing—a process referred to as "infiltration." In one section of the Black Belt, the HOLC inspector noted that rents had increased by thirty percent between 1935 and 1940—"but only to colored people." To the south, Washington Park—designed by the legendary landscape architect Frederick Law Olmsted—was "a very fine park," but one "almost completely monopolized by the colored race," the inspector wrote. "Washington Park is already doomed."

All of Bronzeville, like every area with any black presence, real or potential, was rated Hazardous. For many white observers, central cities weren't just physically obsolete and economically weak. They were also racially "doomed."

Official pessimism about the future of American cities led to two different, and somewhat conflicting, responses from the federal government. Each would pose major challenges to the middle-class residents of places like Crilly Court and Carl Street, and would profoundly shape the way they tried to "save" their neighborhoods.

On the one hand, the federal government devoted massive resources to getting middle-class white families to leave urban areas. Beginning with President Franklin Roosevelt's New Deal in the 1930s, Washington offered huge subsidies to white home buyers—as long as they were willing to move to a government-approved home far from older city neighborhoods threatened by apartments and racial "infiltration." One study of Federal Housing Authority-approved mortgages in the Chicago area in the 1930s found that of 374 such mortgages examined, only three were granted for homes in the central city.

Meanwhile, state and local governments redirected their transportation funds to accommodate the automobile. While carmakers played up the freedom of movement private vehicles made possible, this freedom was almost entirely dependent on the number, quality, design, and congestion of publicly financed roads. This quickly became a policy priority. In 1916, Illinois launched a $129 million ($3 billion in 2018 dollars) roadbuilding program, which would create much of the infrastructure that made the mass adoption of driving possible in the Chicago metropolitan area.

But government didn't just underwrite flight to the suburbs. It also increasingly began to look for ways to "improve" inner city neighborhoods. By far the most far-reaching of these efforts was called "slum clearance." Demolishing entire neighborhoods at a time, the government bulldozer loomed as an existential threat for older, lower-income neighborhoods—including Lincoln Park.

Slum clearance was based on the conviction—supported by near consensus among elite urban planners and sociologists—that making older neighborhoods economically viable again was not a question of renovation, but of wiping the slate clean and starting over. It was the traditional urban forms themselves, like apartments built right up to the street, that *caused* older neighborhoods to suffer from what the sociologists called "disorder," like crime or poor health.

To bring the city "up to a tolerable standard of life," wrote Louis Wirth, an influential University of Chicago sociologist, targeted rehabilitation was hopeless: "[Cities] must be reconstructed by the square mile instead of the individual house or city block."

To a great extent, the ideas behind slum clearance would be incubated and pioneered in Chicago. But while local civic and business leaders provided the intellectual and political arguments, city government did not have the resources to carry out clearance on a large scale. Only when the federal government put its funds behind the program did it really take off.

Under the New Deal, massive demolition projects were carried out to make room for new low-income public housing. For many liberal supporters, the opportunity to demolish older neighborhoods through slum clearance was as important as the new homes that would be built on the rubble. In 1934, a coalition of Chicago business and civic leaders who supported clearance and redevelopment created the Metropolitan Housing and Planning Council. Many of its prominent backers had strong incentives to stem the decline of the inner city because they ran difficult-to-move institutions threatened by "blight." For Marshall Field's vice president, it was the great Loop department store; for the president of the Illinois Institute of Technology, it was a South Side campus surrounded by the growing Black Belt.

The MPHC hired a social worker named Elizabeth Wood to lead it. Three years later, Wood was appointed to the leadership of the new Chicago Housing Authority (CHA). At the CHA, Wood endorsed a mandate not just to build public housing, but to sweep aside "obsolete" neighborhoods. The CHA would not build "small projects, islands in a wilderness of slums," she wrote, but work for "comprehensive" redevelopment.

But there were two major problems with using public housing construction as a tool for slum clearance. First, it required large federal subsidies; and second, it required building public housing—which was rapidly becoming a political third rail. Constructing enough public housing to replace all the areas officially deemed slums seemed extremely unlikely. In 1943, the Chicago Plan Commission published a report that found that twenty-three square miles of the city containing 242,000 homes—nearly a quarter of Chicago's housing stock—were physically "blighted" and would need to be rebuilt. Another 100,000 homes were "substandard" and might soon be beyond repair. Much of Lincoln Park was covered by these designations.

Few civic leaders believed that replacing such a large swath of the city with public housing was desirable—let alone financially or politically possible. But some people believed it might be easier to carry out government slum clearance if it were followed by private, for-profit redevelopment.

The Metropolitan Housing and Planning Council led the charge. As early as 1942, MHPC began to craft model legislation that would allow governments to seize land, demolish the existing buildings, and sell the land at a "write-down" to private developers who would rebuild in ways more palatable to the middle class.

In 1947, the Illinois legislature passed the Redevelopment and Relocation Acts, which gave Chicago exactly those powers. The CHA—which under Elizabeth Wood's leadership had gained a reputation for being a little too eager to build racially integrated public housing—was replaced as the primary engine of slum clearance by the new Chicago Land Clearance Commission. Two years later, President Truman signed the Housing Act of 1949, which took much of the model of Illinois' slum clearance laws and enacted them on a federal level.

The Land Clearance Commission wasted little time in exercising its vast powers. Soon, planning had begun for clearance of a vast swath of Bronzeville, to be redeveloped as modernist high-rises by the New York Life Insurance Company. Over the next few years, the city would spend nearly three million dollars to clear an area of more than a quarter square mile, and then sell the land to New York Life for $500,000. At least 3,500 households, almost all of them black, were displaced; few were able to return to the new private homes that rented for as much as six times more than what had been torn down. Those who did return found that every physical trace of the neighborhood they had known had been eliminated.

———————

The white middle class who had settled around Crilly Court and Carl Street watched what was happening in Chicago's urban core with trepidation. Each trend seemed to represent an existential threat to their small community on the North Side. The ongoing exodus of their friends to the suburbs might leave them adrift in the growing slums; any hint of "infiltration" from the small black community nearby would only speed up that process. And if the neighborhood didn't improve to the Land Clearance Commission's liking, their homes and schools and churches might all be bulldozed into oblivion.

And yet rather than move to safer territory, these rehabbers spent the 1940s organizing community groups that would lay the foundation for decades of struggle to reshape and redefine the neighborhood—at great cost in time, effort, and money. Why did they do this? And why were these groups led by middle-class newcomers, rather than longer-term residents?

One obvious answer is that most of the people who had spent more time in those communities did try to make improvements, but lacked the money to rehabilitate buildings or the political capital to lobby City Hall or Washington on their behalf. In many ways, of course, it was the area's longer-term residents who were most vulnerable if they were pushed to leave the neighborhood: the ones who were too old or financially unstable to move; the ones who couldn't afford the car they would need in the suburbs; the ones who depended on nearby friends and family for childcare or transportation or other day-to-day necessities.

But surveys also suggested that many of these Lincoln Parkers *did* aspire to climb what had become the prescribed social ladder up and out of the central city to more modern and well-tended neighborhoods on the city's edge or in the suburbs. Unlike the residents of Bronzeville, for whom displacement meant a brutal hunt for housing hemmed in by rocks and Molotov cocktails, these overwhelmingly white Chicagoans had access to any part of the metropolitan area they could afford. And the context of a big American city in the 1940s, an aspirational life almost by definition meant one farther from downtown. Finally, government policy ensured that "moving up" in the central city was particularly difficult for people of more modest means. Those who needed federal mortgage programs to purchase a home had to go where the government made those programs available: the suburbs.

Still, most people with enough wealth to buy property on their own were also headed out of the central city. What was new about the young couples on Crilly Court and the artists and their friends on Carl Street was that they began to insist that the comforts and privileges of middle-class American suburbs could be brought to—and enhanced by—their inner city surroundings.

At the very least, they argued, the shorter commutes to downtown meant a more relaxed, dignified life. Chicago Historical Society director Paul Angle, who bought a home near Crilly Court, teased his fellow professionals with big lawns in front of big houses: "The poor devils in Glenview or Hinsdale or Beverly Hills are breaking their necks to catch a train…. I take a short nap [and] enjoy a leisurely breakfast at the same time as commuters who left homes while I was still in bed."

But people like Angle also saw their city neighborhood as a richer, more authentic kind of community. That had long been the ethos of the artists' studios on Carl and Wells Streets. Increasingly, it was also a guiding principle behind the more traditional renovations taking place on Crilly Court and nearby blocks, where old Victorian facades were an intentional statement of opposition to the uniformity of modern tract housing in the suburbs and the cold anonymity of downtown high-rises. Another early rehabber described the mix of counterculture and middle-class improvement projects as "a combination of Greenwich Village and the PTA."

These newcomers also believed they benefited from the presence of the neighborhood's longer-term residents. Unlike the white flight suburbs, the inner North Side included people from a range of class and ethnic backgrounds. While it was overwhelmingly white, it was also home to a community of Assyrians who had fled persecution around World War I, as well as Japanese-Americans who had migrated to Chicago after being released from federal internment, founding a Buddhist temple near Crilly Court in 1944. "Kids will grow up with broader horizons for having lived" in Lincoln Park, wrote one early middle-class arrival, explaining why he chose to settle in the neighborhood.

These new residents also reinterpreted the area's aging homes and storefronts. Rather than holding the neighborhood back, as HOLC's inspectors thought, the frame cottages and brick townhomes dating back to the 1870s represented a rich heritage they might now inherit. Even as their current working class occupants contributed an earthy authenticity, the pedigree of the homes themselves linked the neighborhood to a elegant, aristocratic past. "Normal residential communities no longer exist on Prairie or Ashland," one community group wrote, referencing the long-gone wealthy districts. "Yet in Lincoln Park the old homes still stand." A 1947 *Chicago Daily News* article described the process of renovation as a restoration of the past: "It won't be long...before Chicago's North Side will begin to look like something out of a well-preserved lithograph."

In addition to invoking the prestige of the past, these new residents also used their neighborhood's historic architecture to link themselves to what they saw as their peer communities around the country. "New York has Greenwich Village, New Orleans its romantic French Quarter," the *Daily News* wrote in a formula that would be used dozens of times in the coming years. "But Chicago may soon begin to boast of its own 'Old Town.'" These comparisons lent the neighborhood's incipient middle-class rebirth the validation of a national movement and the cachet of iconic neighborhoods in coastal cities.

According to this new vision, Chicago's "Old Town"—the new name boosters gave the southeast corner of Lincoln Park where rehabbing was concentrated—was a kind of Goldilocks neighborhood. It had the authenticity and diversity of the working class inner city without its hopeless poverty; the culture and convenience of downtown with the neighborliness of the suburbs; the creative sophistication of New York in the heart of the Midwest. It was, in other words, a neighborhood worth defending.

The rehabbers' efforts to take up that defense started small. The freewheeling Burton Place (the new name for Carl Street, which the city had changed in 1936) arts community of the early 1940s buckled down enough to form a block club whose dues-paying members met the first Monday of every month to discuss neighborhood issues and assign housekeeping tasks like litter pickup, snow shoveling, and tree pruning. When some residents felt the street was too dark at night, they successfully lobbied the city for a new street lamp. The message was clear: Burton Place wouldn't tolerate the superficial "disorder" that defined outsiders' views of inner city neighborhoods.

During World War II, civil defense associations gave a new boost to community organization in the southeast corner of Lincoln Park around Crilly Court. This area—bordered by North Avenue on the south, the lake on the east, and diagonal Ogden Avenue on the north and west—came to be known as "the Triangle." Neighbors organized victory gardens (vegetable plots meant to ease wartime produce shortages) and a playground. Edgar Crilly, as part of his ongoing efforts to upgrade his property, lent financial support to these projects.

The most durable organizations were founded after the war, however. In November 1945, a group of residents on Orleans Street met to figure out what to do about unattended children causing trouble. The next spring, the Menomonee Club for Boys—named after a street that ran through the Triangle—opened its clubhouse in a vacant storefront stocked with ping pong tables, board games, and equipment to screen weekly movies. The Club quickly found support from the Triangle's most connected and resourced residents, and began raising the $1,500 needed to buy its own building.

Two years later, in 1948, many of the same people who had supported the Menomonee Club met again to launch a more wide-ranging neighborhood improvement effort. This new organization would address many of the public housekeeping issues that the Burton Place association had dealt with, but it was also meant to go further. It would try to overcome the area's redlining by convincing banks to issue mortgages to local homebuyers; it would lobby the city to change street patterns to keep away the heavy traffic that threatened residential quiet; and it would file official complaints against landlords who didn't keep their buildings up to code. It would, in other words, take on the holistic task of bringing the neighborhood up to its new residents' standards—and, the club founders hoped, up to the standards of the banks and the Land Clearance Commission.

The new neighborhood organization called itself the Old Town Triangle Association (OTTA). Appropriately, they chose as their first president a man named James Beverly, who had bought three buildings on Lincoln Avenue for $14,500 in 1946 and then spent more than four times that amount to renovate them. Beverly's day job was at Marshall Field's, where he bought antiques to be salvaged, dusted off, and resold.

OTTA had reasons to be ambitious. At the end of the 1940s, the United States was throwing itself into some of the most far-reaching urban transformations in the history of the world. The end of the war meant that a decade-plus of pent up demand for housing could finally be met with a massive wave of construction. At the same time, city centers were beginning to see government-led urban renewal projects demolish and rebuild entire neighborhoods.

On the other hand, it was increasingly clear that very few of the vast resources being thrown into these transformations might actually help Old Town. New construction, with the help of government mortgages and highways, was mostly taking place in the suburbs. HOLC had ruled that the Old Town Triangle was too "Hazardous" to receive government-backed loans, and private banks weren't eager to finance new purchases or rehabilitations either. And in 1950, urban renewal meant slum clearance, which meant tearing down all the old buildings that OTTA's members had lovingly restored.

In other words, there was money for brand new neighborhoods—either out in suburban farmland or on the rubble of a cleared slum—but there wasn't money to preserve a neighborhood like Old Town.

Lacking external support, the rehabbers sought to raise funds themselves. And so, on a June afternoon in 1950, they hung everything from oil paintings to crocheted potholders on fences and tables set up along Lincoln Park West. St. Michael's Church set up a refreshment table; the Buddhist temple offered chicken teriyaki. And the Old Town Triangle Association sold tickets to the festival, raising money for the Menomonee Club.

The grand total from the first annual Old Town Holiday art fair was just $400. Nevertheless, it marked an important milestone for the neighborhood organization. Like the art fairs on Burton Street a decade earlier, the Old Town Holiday was a "tangible, prestigious project" that "could establish the identity" of the community to outsiders, explained one organizer. And it would build a sense of pride among the neighbors who had organized it, "weld[ing] them into an effective organization which could deal with the diverse and changing challenges facing the area they called home."

But if the Old Town Holiday was a stepping stone, there needed to be something else to step towards. Fortunately for the rehabbers, policymakers were already working on a new version of "urban renewal" that they would find more palatable.

The idea of "conservation" had been around for some time by the early 1950s. Like many other urban interventions, some of its roots began with whites looking for a way to keep out black residents while preserving as much as possible of their neighborhoods' physical and social fabric. As early as 1941, the Southtown Planning Association—a group of explicitly segregationist white residents in the South Side community of Englewood—began to put together a plan for the targeted acquisition and redevelopment of a small black pocket there, while leaving the rest of the neighborhood untouched.

A few years later, in another part of the South Side, the Oakland-Kenwood Property Owners' Association sought new strategies for slowing the spread of black Chicagoans after racially restrictive covenants were ruled unconstitutional in 1947. Negotiating with groups like the Urban League and Chicago NAACP, who hoped to avoid the violence and instability that characterized rapid racial change in the city, they came up with "conservation agreements." On their face, these agreements were contracts that would require property owners to perform strict maintenance on their buildings. But the Oakland-Kenwood association clearly hoped they would limit the number of homes available to black tenants or homebuyers.

Meanwhile, downtown civic leaders were promoting their own version of "conservation."

In a pair of speeches to the City Club of Chicago in the early 1950s, Robert Merriam—a former president of the Metropolitan Housing and Planning Council who became an alderman in 1947—laid out his case. It was true, Merriam argued, that almost a quarter of Chicago's homes were in "slum" areas. But it was also true that another *half* of the city was in "good middle-aged areas… which are threatened by spreading blight." While he was in favor of "even greater and more accelerated slum clearance," without dramatic action, Merriam claimed, the slums would spread faster than they could be cleared.

Merriam's conclusions were echoed by members of the Loop business community who felt threatened by the continued economic decline of the central city. Earl Kribben, a vice president at Marshall Field's, warned that poor planning and service provision were pushing "middle-aged residential neighborhoods...rapidly into slums." Kribben also added a business case: Preventing the creation of a slum was up to thirty percent cheaper, he estimated, than clearing one that had already formed.

Moreover, city officials argued, there was reason to believe these "middle" neighborhoods could be revived. In a passage strikingly similar to the Old Towners' pitch for their own community, the Chicago Plan Commission argued that "a substantial type of citizen" could be lured back if Chicago's neighborhoods were able to "provide many of the advantages of suburban communities plus the advantage of being within walking distance of places of employment, stores, theaters, parks, museums, and libraries."

Just as Illinois' 1947 slum clearance law was supercharged by the passage of a federal slum clearance act in 1949, Illinois legislators pioneered their own conservation act in 1953, providing a framework for an even more powerful national conservation policy the very next year.

The state Urban Community Conservation Act, which the Metropolitan Housing and Planning Council had essentially drafted in 1952, dramatically expanded the government's powers to seize property. Now, not just slum *clearance*, but slum *prevention* would legally justify taking and redeveloping land. Under the Act, cities could designate neighborhoods at risk of becoming slums as "conservation areas." After the designation, a local council would be appointed to create detailed plans for zoning, traffic, and targeted clearance.

The federal Housing Act of 1954 put billions of dollars of federal money behind local conservation efforts. Washington pledged to cover up to two-thirds of the costs of conservation programs, which were supposed to emphasize smaller-scale demolition and the rehabilitation of older buildings. On top of that, neighborhoods with an official conservation program would be given the same privileged terms on government-backed mortgages as newer suburbs, reversing the damage of HOLC's redlining.

The rehabbers in and around Old Town did not wait for City Hall or Washington to come to them. In March of 1953, the Old Town Triangle Association led a coalition of organizations from the larger Lincoln Park area—mostly from the eastern edge along the lake, where a few other professional-class pockets had grown in the otherwise working-class community—in asking a Chicago housing official to brief them on how Lincoln Park might take advantage of the new urban conservation laws.

A year later, residents of Old Town and Lincoln Park received an invitation in the mail. It was from a new organization called the Lincoln Park Conservation Association, and it wanted them to come to a meeting.

"Lincoln Park is unique," LPCA wrote. "It is the best close-in residential area. It can be protected against the decay of neglect by insistence on the full share of municipal services to which it is entitled." And, the letter explained, new conservation laws meant that the time had come to demand their "full share," and to "resist anything which encroaches on our residential pattern."

"You are at the beginning," the letter concluded. "With your help we will plot the future of the Lincoln Park area."

The name was new, but the people behind LPCA were not: The very first name on the letter was Edgar Crilly's. Below his were James Beverly, OTTA's first president, and Pierre Blouke, OTTA's new president, along with more than a dozen notable Old Town residents, local business and religious leaders, and representatives of local hospitals and DePaul University.

"We are convinced there is enough interest, talent, and money among our neighbors to restore the area," LPCA wrote. Lincoln Parkers quickly proved their interest, as more than 150 people turned out to the first meeting in March. Money, too, came soon: Crilly made a founding donation of $1,000, and offered to lease one of his storefronts—just a block from the Wells Street artist studios Sol Kogen, Edgar Miller, and Jesus Torres had begun renovating almost twenty years before—as LPCA's first office for a dollar. OTTA, for its part, pledged $100 per month.

But LPCA's leadership believed their work depended almost entirely on the confidence, planning resources, and funds that would come with designation as an official conservation area. Ultimately, their application would have to be approved by federal urban renewal officials. The first step, though, was to convince Chicago's mayor and city council, who would forward the application to Washington. So LPCA's lobbying campaign began.

To grow the Association's membership, they canvassed door-to-door, passed out flyers, and took out ads in local newspapers. By the end of 1954, they had over 200 members, each of whom paid $10 for the privilege. Many joined one of the growing list of LPCA committees tasked with diagnosing problems and designing solutions for particular subjects like Housing Standards, Schools, and Crime.

Throughout 1955, they held meetings with major city planning figures to plot their course. Frederick Aschman, the Executive Director of the Chicago Plan Commission, suggested hiring paid staff. Richard Smykal, Building Commissioner, spoke of the importance of building inspections, and warned about the blight of rooming houses. Raymond Spaeth, the president of the Illinois Institute of Technology and the South Side Planning Board, which was undertaking some of the city's most ambitious urban renewal projects in Bronzeville and the University of Chicago's Hyde Park, contrasted the complete demolition of the "totally deteriorated slum" that had been Lake Meadows with the "selectivity" that would be required on the North Side.

LPCA's public relations campaign continued as well. The organization began to distribute a monthly newsletter, which explained the conservation process and LPCA's vision for a transformed neighborhood. The November 1955 issue included perhaps the most vivid imagining of a "renovated" Lincoln Park: a "letter from the future," in which a Lincoln Parker from 1975 took the reader on a walking tour of the last twenty years' changes.

In one direction, a busy commercial thoroughfare had been transformed into "quiet, leafy Clark Parkway with its shops and landscaped parking lots." In another, a "well-planned shopping plaza" boasted a "famous restaurant." In between, they pointed to "architecturally significant additions" to schools, a park with a fountain "dedicated to our children's pets," and an antique shopping district known as "Antiquarians' Mecca"—all nestled onto clean, well-maintained streets.

How had these changes come to pass? A reader in 1955 might have known about the growing protests against renewal and clearance projects elsewhere in the city, and wondered if they would face similar resistance. The "letter from the future" was coy about this possibility: the conservation process itself, the author wrote, "is now light-heartedly referred to as 'the Battle of Lincoln Park.'"

PART TWO

THE CONSERVATION OF LINCOLN PARK

1956-1964

CHAPTER 3
STRICT ENFORCEMENT

In June 1956, on a sweltering "Turkish bath-type summer evening," Chicago's Community Conservation Board heard dozens of LPCA supporters testify in the auditorium of Lincoln Park's Waller High School. A short time later, the Board voted to make Lincoln Park the city's third official conservation area, after the University of Chicago's Hyde Park on the South Side, and a Near West Side district that would become the University of Illinois at Chicago's new campus.

The vote marked a new phase in the rehabbers' campaign to remake the neighborhood. After two years of work, LPCA's leadership believed the immense powers that came with conservation status—the ability to seize, demolish, renovate, and rebuild dilapidated buildings blocks at a time—would supercharge their efforts beyond what private renovations could accomplish. And they expected to control those powers through the official local advisory body, the Lincoln Park Conservation Community Council, which would be appointed by Mayor Richard Daley.

But these expectations would—at least temporarily—be dashed. With fierce competition for limited funds, the federal resources the rehabbers hoped to use were still nearly a decade away.

Yet even without those resources, the pace of physical and social change in Lincoln Park accelerated dramatically over the following years. In part, this was because the rehabbers discovered new advantages that came simply from being *labeled* a conservation area. But they also found that private investors had far more power to change the neighborhood than they had anticipated—and not always in ways they approved of.

At the same time, these accelerating changes also brought attention to LPCA from other Lincoln Parkers who weren't part of the rehabbing movement. These neighbors—who still made up the vast majority of residents in most parts of the community—raised growing concerns that rehabbing was squeezing them out of their own homes.

As a result, the rehabbers found themselves with a fight on three fronts. Their campaign to eliminate "blight" in Lincoln Park continued, but they also fought to gain control over the private investors who threatened the neighborhood character they prized, even as they tried to fend off the growing number of Lincoln Parkers who felt the same way about them.

———————

Almost immediately after being certified as a conservation district, LPCA sent Mayor Daley a list of names for appointment to Lincoln Park's Conservation Community Council, which the law said the city had to create to oversee planning for the program. But Daley, who was more politically interested in the conservation programs in Hyde Park and the Near West Side, declined to appoint anyone to Lincoln Park's Council at all. At first, the rehabbers were taken aback. Quickly, however, they came to understand that their new status as a conservation area had value on its own. And by the late 1950s, LPCA executive director Malcolm Shanower would brag that "conservation is moving ahead with private capital, without waiting for federal aid."

LPCA helped to push that private capital along. In an attempt "to attract new and desirable residents to the area," it set up a property referral service to match available homes with people looking to move into Lincoln Park. At an August 1956 board meeting—barely a month after the City Council vote—staff reported that "prospective tenants are prepared to pay fairly substantial rentals so long as they were in the conservation area."

Why were newcomers willing to pay a premium to live in a designated conservation area, even if the conservation program only existed on paper? For many people, conservation status signaled that the community would be stabilized, and that their investments in housing there would be safe, both socially—conservation status attracted middle-class home buyers, who wanted to be around other middle-class home buyers—and financially. Rehabbers usually bought their homes for far less than they would have paid in the suburbs, but often poured two or three times the cost into renovations. If the building's resale value didn't increase proportionally, they faced an enormous loss. And the resale value wouldn't increase unless there were more and more middle-class buyers.

To assure potential renovators of a future market, then, OTTA and LPCA realized that it was important for their area to be *perceived* as "up and coming." Middle-class people would only purchase homes in places that they believed other middle-class people would purchase homes. That was the immediate value of the conservation designation: "It gave people confidence," as one resident put it, "that the area was going to be maintained."

As rehabbing picked up steam, it expanded out from the established strongholds like Crilly Court in Old Town. Artists and other bohemians formed a kind of advance front, searching for a Tower Town-like middle ground. One artist described their ideal: "Just different enough to be interesting but not in a state of decline...a safe frontier...just fringe enough."

The more affluent buyers, however, formed a tight circle that grew block by block behind them. People willing to buy on a block just outside the established renovation areas could find the best deals, but they also faced the prospect—which seemed entirely realistic even in the late 1950s—that others wouldn't follow, particularly if they strayed too far. "I remember someone living on Sheffield," one rehabber recalled. "I thought they were in the woods that was so far away." As a result, they often tried to recruit their friends to buy on their block, fulfilling their own expectations. It only took a few conspicuously rehabbed homes to open the floodgates.

"The first two or three or four are the ones taking the risk," one real estate agent reflected. "After that, zoom."

Much of OTTA's and LPCA's work was meant to facilitate this process. They lobbied local banks to make mortgage and home improvement loans, concentrating on particular blocks they wanted to "turn." To build confidence in the general area, they worked to spread the word about the coming conservation program. And they held public events to showcase the neighborhood.

Visitors to the Old Town Holiday fair—which had grown in attendance from 4,000 in 1950 to 36,000 by 1956—didn't just gawk at the watercolor canvases, but at the nearby homes with their fresh paint and tuckpointing. For those who needed a prod, OTTA volunteers painted white footprints from the heart of the fair to particularly charming side streets, encouraging visitors to see the new planted window boxes and landscaped patio gardens in a neighborhood that many middle-class white Chicagoans still considered questionable.

The rehabbers were changing more than peeling paint and undecorated windows. Though they may have been conserving the physical infrastructure of the neighborhood from decay or demolition, they were also setting in motion profound changes in its social infrastructure. Specifically, as LPCA worked to make the neighborhood more livable for the kind of middle-class white families that might otherwise have fled to the suburbs, they often did so in ways that directly threatened the homes or livelihoods of their poor and working-class neighbors.

The rehabbers were often quite explicit in connecting their work on physical rehabilitation with social rehabilitation, and the relationship between the kind of homes they desired to live among and the kind of people they desired to have as neighbors. This tendency stood in tension to their professed commitment to Lincoln Park's social diversity, a contradiction most rehabbers had a hard time confronting in the 1950s.

In fact, the leadership of LPCA and OTTA attempted to reconcile these priorities. "True conservation necessarily requires not only the rehabilitation of structures," one LPCA publication said in 1956, "but the rehabilitation rather than the elimination of social groups." Rehabbers expressed great concern about the threat of displacement by urban renewal. "One of the great mistakes in Lake Meadows [in Bronzeville]," an LPCA newsletter wrote after City Council certification, "was that a large area was wrecked without considering where the people who lived there were going." To make the same mistake in Lincoln Park, it concluded, would be "inexcusable." And even in private communications, rehabbers both in and out of leadership posts cited the area's economic, generational, and ethnic diversity as one of its best attributes.

Yet LPCA's vision for the neighborhood clearly privileged a narrower range of people. Sometimes, this was framed in terms of "new" versus "old" residents. Often, as in a 1956 pamphlet called "History of Lincoln Park and the Conservation Program," the organization referred vaguely to the beneficial influence of newcomers with "high community standards," as compared with "older residents, who had been neglecting their properties." The pamphlet did not mention that these residents had been barred from taking out home improvement loans because of redlining, or that most did not have the personal wealth to undertake major renovations themselves.

Not surprisingly, LPCA had few of these "older residents" as members. In a 1959 survey, just thirteen percent of LPCA members listed "grew up in the area" as a reason for living in Lincoln Park. Malcolm Shanower, who had been involved in the founding of LPCA, later lamented to an interviewer how hard he felt it had been for the organization "to get any of the old-timers"—predominantly working-class whites—"to be the least bit interested." Throughout the 1950s, LPCA's "leadership…came from people who had been in the community less than ten years."

That recruitment problem probably had something to do with the beliefs rehabbers had about what made a "good" resident. In particular, the rehabbers prioritized homeownership, and especially the ownership of single-family houses. In an area where eighty-five percent of households rented, more than seventy percent of LPCA members owned their own home. And for many rehabbers, homeownership wasn't simply a prudent financial choice; it was a social and civic virtue. The Victorian buildings they valued couldn't reach their full potential, fully reclaim their "dignity and charm," until they had been "restored to single-family use." Where Sol Kogen, Edgar Miller, and Jesus Torres had tried to make something experimental and communal out of the pieces of old buildings, these new rehabbers believed themselves to be re-establishing the historic, domestic character their buildings were meant to have.

If the ideal home was a single-family house, the ideal household was a single nuclear family. OTTA's materials explained that "the renewal of Old Town was based on a recognition of the inherent value of a low-density, family-oriented residential community close to the center of a great city." LCPA's 1955 "letter from the future" predicted that conservation would deliver an "uncrowded family environment." And an official publication from 1956 declared that "many of the goals of LPCA…serve to attract an even greater proportion of" "the most responsible and civic-minded young families."

But whether or not they acknowledged it, creating this "uncrowded" environment would require removing the "crowds." The priority of traditional families in spacious homes would have seemed obvious to the rehabbers' educated, middle-class contacts in postwar suburbs. But it did not reflect the household structures, or financial capabilities, of most of their inner city neighbors. To be sure, there were many parents, children, and grandparents among the older residents of Old Town and Lincoln Park. But the vast majority of them rented, many in smaller apartments that had been carved out of larger spaces.

Indeed, in Old Town and Lincoln Park, less than one in twenty homes was configured as a single-family house in 1950. (In 2015, the figure was nearly one in five.) Many apartments were "rooming houses," in which renters—often single workers, young people, or the elderly, who together made up about a third of all Old Town households—paid for a bedroom with communal bath and kitchen facilities. These modest accommodations made finding affordable housing in a close-in neighborhood possible for lower-income people.

Rehabbing nearly always meant eliminating these smaller homes by combining them into something considered more appropriate by a white, middle-class family. Many of the Carl Street artist conversions in the 1920s and 30s had evicted low-income tenants from rooming houses to make space for their creative reinventions; many buyers of the 1950s found themselves doing the same before taking on more traditional renovations.

Importantly, the elimination of small apartments and rooming houses was not just collateral damage: it was a major goal in itself. In general, proponents of urban renewal considered these homes and the people who lived in them a threat to the desirability of urban neighborhoods: "When one house is converted from a single-family house to a multi-family dwelling," a Chicago renewal tract from 1955 warned, "it will not be long before blight sets in and extends to other houses."

To prevent this outcome, OTTA and LPCA created what became known as the "strict enforcement campaign." Staff and members were encouraged to identify buildings with apartment conversions that appeared to violate zoning or building codes, and LPCA would sue to have them deconverted. To be sure, many converted buildings in Lincoln Park, and in the rest of the city, did pose real health and safety concerns. But LPCA's approach almost always involved evicting current tenants without finding them new, higher-quality homes. Instead, evicted tenants were expected to find new apartments elsewhere in the city, where they would likely either face higher rents or similar building code issues.

Each month's newsletter detailed the latest legal battles. An April 1958 issue declared a "smashing victory" in securing the demolition of a three-story brick building and the "eviction of the undesirable tenants." In another, under a headline that read "LPCA scores again!", the organization celebrated a judge's order to "vacate all occupants" from two buildings, which were then to be deconverted into larger, "attractive apartments." Of the evicted tenants, the article noted that they "moved in and out at strange hours" and held "immoral parties."

LPCA's staff noted that these tactics caused some dissent within the neighborhood. "A significant number of old residents… came in to voice their anxiety about demolition [and] strict building code enforcement," an August 1957 newsletter reported. But it warned readers away from sympathy. In fact, the newsletter explained, it was these residents who threatened the rehabbers, not the other way around: "Pockets of non-members and non-sympathizers, especially in small or old buildings, are dangerous vacuums for a shift to blight." Confronted with actual complaints of displacement, the rehabbers' sensitivities shrank before their drive to remake Lincoln Park.

Meanwhile, there was still little official conservation to speak of.

Before the City Council vote in the summer of 1956, LPCA had hoped to have "all aspects of the program implemented and past 50 percent completion" by the end of 1959. It did not take long to understand this timeline was impossible. Competing with conservation areas in Hyde Park-Kenwood, backed by the powerful University of Chicago, and the Near West Side, where Mayor Daley would put the new University of Illinois at Chicago campus, LPCA leadership complained their requests for funds were pushed to the back of the line. These higher-priority conservation programs meant that nothing was left over for Lincoln Park: In 1958, Chicago had $209 million more in conservation proposals than available federal funds.

Yet Chicago's local courts had picked up the slack where the federal government had failed to appear. Court-ordered renovations, demolitions, and evictions had proven invaluable for the strict enforcement campaign, changing Lincoln Park's housing stock in ways that the rehabbers would have been unable to do on their own. And major urban renewal projects in other parts of the city would soon affect the fate of Lincoln Park as well.

Washington-led urban renewal may have been slow coming to Lincoln Park, but it was galloping through the rest of the city. Between 1948 and 1958, highways, public and private housing, and other public works led to the seizure and demolition of more than 40,000 homes in Chicago.

These projects, most of which targeted the South and West Sides, sometimes seemed to be worlds away from the Victorian renovations in Lincoln Park. But in fact LPCA's work was tightly interconnected with renewal elsewhere in the city. Rehabbers had to fight for limited resources with places like Hyde Park, of course. But they also knew that the success of their campaign to reinvent their neighborhood depended on what happened in the rest of Chicago.

For starters, one of Lincoln Park's main advantages—its proximity to the Loop—depended crucially on efforts to improve downtown shopping and cultural offerings while staving off "blight." Middle class whites' confidence in the neighborhood's future also relied on its relative isolation from the city's black population, which in turn depended on the city's use of highways and public housing to enforce segregation on the South Side. The fact that black residents arrived to the North Side in much smaller numbers helped to drive much of the private capital that was transforming the neighborhood. "Lincoln Park had to be the next area," one real estate investor told a researcher. "The near north was already heavily built up, and the values were not there. Some of us looked to the South Shore-Hyde Park area. But the number of blacks...made such investments untenable."

Two renewal projects in the Near North Side community just south of Lincoln Park demonstrate how developments in the rest of the city profoundly challenged and assisted the rehabbers' agenda. One, a massive expansion of public housing in the area formerly known as "Little Hell," created a seemingly permanent pocket of poor black and Puerto Rican people just south of Lincoln Park, which the rehabbers would attempt to keep isolated from their own areas. The other, a huge middle-class renewal project barricading the western flank of the Gold Coast, protected the downtown wealth Lincoln Park depended on—but also displaced thousands of low-income people, including large numbers of Puerto Ricans and Appalachians, many of whom settled in Lincoln Park. Their sudden arrival dramatically changed the character of the conservation movement for the next decade and more.

The Chicago Housing Authority opened the Francis Cabrini row homes in the district formerly known as "Little Hell" in the Near North Side in 1942, hoping the neat public homes would help upgrade the surrounding area. Instead, the low-rent area continued to expand east, towards Michigan Avenue and the Gold Coast, and north towards Lincoln Park.

Fueled by the Second Great Migration from the South, which took off during World War II, the area's small black population was also growing rapidly. In 1940, the Near North Side had been home to about 5,100 black Chicagoans; by 1950, the number had tripled to 17,800. The Cabrini row homes, which CHA Executive Director Elizabeth Wood tried to maintain integrated with a twenty percent black quota, became segregated as white households refused to live in the area. Back in the 1920s, the *Tribune* had warned that Little Hell might become the seed of another "black belt" on the North Side. Now that prophecy seemed to be coming true.

The city, working with private businesses, launched two very different renewal projects to head off this possibility.

The first demolished nearly all of what remained of Little Hell to expand public housing around the Cabrini row homes. The new Cabrini Extension and William Green Homes would hold 3,000 units in twenty-three modernist towers, widely spaced on land that had been filled with small, tightly packed walkup apartments. The first fifteen buildings officially opened in 1958, with the remainder scheduled for 1961.

The new Cabrini-Green complex represented, at least for a while, a more modern vision of low-income housing. But because whites were rapidly abandoning Chicago's public housing in the 1950s, it also locked in a large black community just to the south of Lincoln Park. Many white Lincoln Parkers, including many rehabbers, felt this community threatened their own in a variety of ways.

Likewise, to the east of the new public housing highrises, city planners, Gold Coast residents, and downtown businessmen watched the easterly spread of low-income and black Chicagoans with trepidation. One of the businessmen, a real estate tycoon named Arthur Rubloff, began to formulate a plan to deal with it.

Rubloff had an especial interest in the Near North Side. In 1948, he had "donated" to the city an ambitious plan for North Michigan Avenue, imagining a "Magnificent Mile" that would be the region's new premier shopping destination. He intended to build, and profit from, many of the planned developments. But he worried that the closer rooming houses and black or other stigmatized people came to Michigan Avenue, the fewer middle-class white people would feel comfortable shopping there, and the less profit there would be.

With a coalition of other businesses, Rubloff presented the city with a new plan. It centered not on Michigan Avenue, but Clark Street, six blocks west and north.

In the 1950s, Clark Street formed a kind of transitional neighborhood between the opulence of the Gold Coast and the deep poverty around the Cabrini row homes. Close to downtown restaurants and theaters, but full of small, cheap apartments—almost half had just one room—the area had attracted several communities of service workers looking for cheap housing close to their jobs. Appalachian migrants, as well as Japanese-Americans released from federal internment camps, came in the 1940s, joining a black community gradually moving in from the Cabrini homes area to the west. During and after World War II, the area also became home to many of the Mexican and Puerto Rican workers who were coming to Chicago as a result of federal programs that encouraged migrant labor. By the mid-1950s, "La Clark" was one of the city's largest Latino communities.

For Rubloff and the North Michigan Avenue Association, La Clark was an unfortunately dingy neighbor. Worse, they feared it might soon become a part of the growing high-poverty, largely black neighborhood spreading east from the Cabrini area, bringing a deeply stigmatized community practically to Michigan Avenue's doorstep. Wouldn't it be better, Rubloff asked, to replace La Clark with middle-class housing that, by design, would remain middle-class? The city's planning department—which had already conducted studies declaring the entire area blighted, and which was deeply concerned with maintaining downtown property values and the tax revenue they provided—agreed that it would.

In accordance with the conventional planning wisdom of the time, the plan's supporters believed that any new middle-class development would have to be massive enough to physically overwhelm older, lower-income areas nearby. John Cordwell, Director of the Chicago Plan Commission, compared the project to an earlier phase of American history: "You can't survive in a wagon completely surrounded by angry Indians," he wrote. "And you can't build an urban renewal project in an area completely surrounded by blight."

The final plan did, in fact, achieve a monumental scale. The city agreed to evict nearly a thousand households by clearing virtually every building along both sides of a half-mile stretch of Clark, as well as some surrounding blocks. The winning bid for redevelopment—predictably, from Rubloff—envisioned a sprawling complex of nearly 2,000 apartments in highrises and townhomes facing interior courtyards. While rents around La Clark averaged barely $70 a month (about $600 in 2018 dollars), Rubloff proposed starting at $115 for studio apartments and reach $215 for larger, family-size units (about $1,000 to $1,800 in 2018 dollars).

In a nod to the artistic reputation of the Old Town Triangle, which sat across the street from the northern end of the project, Rubloff gave his project a literary theme. Individual towers were given names like Faulkner, Cummings, and Dickinson. The entire complex would be named Carl Sandburg Village, after the poet who had given Chicago its "broad shoulders" moniker.

———————————

The first tenants didn't move into Sandburg Village until 1963, but Old Town and Lincoln Park began to feel the effect of the project as the city seized and demolished homes along La Clark in 1958. Many of the displaced households simply moved north to the cheaper housing in Lincoln Park's western half.

The attitude of many rehabbers to their new neighbors was summed up by one woman describing the changes on a block near Halsted: "Bissell [Street] attracted people down on their luck, the dregs of society. The people were poor, with problems. There were Puerto Rican renters, Appalachians…. The rest defied description, but they are all low-income, low-education."

As this quote suggests, two groups in particular raised eyebrows among the rehabbers. First were the southern and Appalachian whites, who were stigmatized as outsiders despite their race and American-born status. "LPCA will have to have more members and more support," a newsletter article on Sandburg Village concluded, "if it is to protect the area from an overflow of honky-tonk dwellers."

But it was the Puerto Rican community forming around Armitage and Halsted streets in the heart of Lincoln Park that would cause the most angst for Anglo whites. In a city defined by its division between white and black, Puerto Ricans and other Latinos occupied uncertain racial ground: not shunned from housing as African-Americans were, but heavily stigmatized and discriminated against—particularly those with darker skin.

The construction of Sandburg Village didn't just push Appalachians and Puerto Ricans into Lincoln Park. It also blockaded the Gold Coast and Michigan Avenue from the spread of the low-rent, racially mixed neighborhood around Cabrini-Green. Nearly all of Lincoln Park and Old Town, however, were left on the low-rent side of the blockade, facing an increasingly black and low-income neighborhood to the south. North Avenue—an old, crowded street of butchers and taverns topped by apartments—became a precarious racial boundary just one block from Crilly Court.

For the first time, LPCA had to face the prospect of real racial integration—and their members' responses to it. In October 1958, a member paying his dues at the Wells Street office confided to Malcolm Shanower that he knew what LPCA was really for. Even if they "can't say it," the man said, he knew "LPCA is really here to see that the negroes are kept out of the community," and he was recruiting his neighbors to join the fight.

The organization's white leaders, who prized their identity as liberal cosmopolitans, blanched. At its next meeting, LPCA's board unanimously passed its first statement on integration, declaring that Lincoln Park was open to all "men and women of good will regardless of color, race, or creed."

Life on the ground in Lincoln Park, however, did not always live up to those ideals.

CHAPTER 4
THE SPECIAL SITUATION

By 1960, anyone paying attention knew that major changes were afoot in Lincoln Park. The Census carried out that year confirmed it.

In terms of income, the changes were perhaps surprisingly modest. Lincoln Park had been the fifteenth poorest of Chicago's seventy-five community areas in 1950, and had slipped slightly to the nineteenth poorest in 1960.

But the headline numbers masked profound social changes on the east side of the neighborhood. While the proportion of all Chicagoans with four-year college degrees remained roughly steady at six percent between 1950 and 1960, in Old Town, it had more than doubled to almost nineteen percent. That made Old Town more highly educated than nine out of ten neighborhoods in the entire Chicago area, including the well-to-do suburbs. The figures were similar all along Lincoln Park's eastern lakefront, from Old Town up through the Mid-North Association's territory. These were now places where white collar workers were a major presence in an overwhelmingly working class city.

The campaign of evictions and deconversions of smaller apartments into larger units also showed up in the Census numbers.

Old Town's population had fallen by more than a sixth—much more than the loss citywide—as new households took up more space than the ones they replaced. Lincoln Park as a whole had seen its population fall from 102,000 to 89,000—again, a much steeper drop than Chicago overall.

The influx of displaced Latino families from La Clark, and the slow spread of black ones from the Cabrini-Green area, was also evident. In 1950, just over 1,800 Lincoln Parkers, or barely over two percent, had Spanish surnames or identified as black (the racial and ethnic breakdowns available in that year's Census). By 1960, that number had grown by 133 percent to over 4,200, even as the number of whites had dropped by 15,000.

This growing racial diversity represented a major change in the social character of the neighborhood. But these headline numbers could also be misleading. Lincoln Park itself, like Chicago, was quite segregated: The vast majority of Latino and black households were in the poorer central or western parts of Lincoln Park, away from the growing middle-class section to the east. Often, Larrabee Street appeared as a kind of border. While one in five adults had a college degree in Old Town, just across Larrabee Street on the Triangle's western side, the proportion was closer to one in forty.

These growing disparities began to raise questions about what kind of neighborhood Lincoln Park was becoming. They also challenged long-accepted neighborhood identities, especially in Old Town. In the 1940s, the founders of the Old Town Triangle Association had praised their neighbors' diversity of age, class, and ethnicity as one of the things that most distinguished their community from the suburbs their peers lived in. But it was becoming harder to recognize the Old Town Triangle as especially diverse.

Partly, that was because of changes within the Triangle itself. As more college-educated families moved in, they reduced the elderly and working-class population by converting rooming houses into single-family homes. At the same time, the Japanese community that had made up most of the area's small non-white population was following the white middle class out to the suburbs.

But the Triangle was perhaps more notable for how it *hadn't* changed. During World War Two, all of Lincoln Park, and the neighborhoods facing it south of North Avenue, had been almost entirely white. In the two decades since then, however, the Near North Side had been transformed by both the Great Migration of black Southerners and the arrival of significant numbers of Puerto Ricans. Much of the area south of North Avenue was now predominantly black; west of Larrabee Street, black and Puerto Rican residents made up as much as a fifth of some parts of Lincoln Park itself.

But east of Larrabee, in the heart of the Triangle, whites still made up well over ninety-five percent of the neighborhood. The lack of integration was conspicuous to liberals who preached the benefits of diversity and took public stances in favor of anti-segregation policies.

At least some believed that their own work might be to blame. "It is fair to characterize the majority of the Triangle residents as integration minded," an OTTA assistant secretary wrote in a 1965 letter. "Though the rent level, because of the success of the operation, has probably been the principal reason for the lack of integration." And yet this conclusion did not lead the bulk of the rehabbers to reevaluate what "success" meant, or what steps they might take to better pursue it.

The racial changes west of Larrabee meant that, even as rehabbing continued to expand outward from Old Town and the lakefront, LPCA's leaders began to consider for the first time the immediate possibility of white flight in the rest of the community. Racial panic had rocked neighborhoods across the South and West Sides in the 1940s and 50s: mobs of whites beat black people accused of integration, firebombed their houses, and rioted in the streets with almost routine frequency. When these efforts failed, white families quickly abandoned their neighborhoods, egged on by real estate agents who looked to buy from fleeing whites at fire sale prices and sell at exorbitantly high ones—and on exploitative terms—to blacks with few other options.

Throughout this period, white liberals in Lincoln Park had mostly been able to observe these campaigns from afar, disapproving without having to navigate any significant integration in their own backyards. But at the start of the 1960s, that was becoming an untenable stance.

Many of the challenges stemmed from the gap between the self-proclaimed racial egalitarianism of LPCA and OTTA leadership, and the actual attitudes of their constituents. The 1958 incident that led to LPCA's first statement of non-discrimination was followed by others. Around the same time, the staffer managing the organization's real estate listing service reported that most of their landlords were requesting no "pets, children, southerners or Puerto Ricans." And LPCA members were increasingly bringing up the presence of Puerto Rican youth as a threat to public safety.

These preoccupations became more intense as the number of Puerto Ricans in the neighborhood grew. In 1962, LPCA assigned a field worker to meet with and organize block clubs in the central and western parts of Lincoln Park, which had fewer of the college-educated professionals who made up the core of its membership along the lake.

He reported back that these block clubs—which were almost exclusively white—were nearly obsessed with race. One group, close to the heart of the Puerto Rican community on Armitage, felt that "the main problem was the race issue," and that city policies were infringing on whites' rights. At another, he wrote, "if the subject of Puerto Ricans is brought up, the meeting progresses no further," because the attendees became too upset to talk about anything else on their agenda.

"There will come a time when this problem will have to be

faced whether the neighborhood wants to or not," he concluded in a memo to LPCA's director, referring to the growing panic over integration among white Lincoln Parkers. "It would be advisable to begin some sort of program which would prepare the neighborhood."

William Friedlander, the Association's new Executive Director, agreed. In a November 1962 report to the board of directors, he wrote that one of LPCA's top priorities was to "create a climate of greater acceptance of non-whites in Lincoln Park."

"Unless it is clearly understood that personal standards, and not ethnic background, are the basis of acceptance in the community," he wrote in another report a two months later, "we could be faced with real panic as inevitable changes occur."

Friedlander's note hinted at the double motivations behind LPCA's strategic embrace of integration. If managed successfully, he believed, the LPCA could trace a middle path between violent resistance and complete abandonment by white families.

Many of the organization's members may have been genuinely committed to civil rights; at least one, the Rev. James Reed, had been involved in citywide organizing efforts against racist real estate practices. But LPCA's leadership also realized that some amount of flexibility on integration was likely the only way to avoid the kind of wholesale racial change that was transforming neighborhoods on the South and West Sides. If Lincoln Parkers believed that "good" neighborhoods must be entirely white, then the arrival of a single black or Puerto Rican family on a block could set off a wave of panicked selling that might destabilize the whole area. But if limited integration were seen as compatible with an "up and coming" community, then there was hope that these self-fulfilling expectations might not take hold.

These calculations were epitomized in a debate over whether to build a new public high school in Lincoln Park. In the early 1960s, the city had proposed a campus north of Waller High School, where enrollment of black and Latino students was growing rapidly. It was clear to everyone that the plan would enable white families to form a new, segregated school, leaving students of color—who mostly came from southern Lincoln Park and the Cabrini-Green area just south of there—at Waller.

LPCA vigorously opposed the segregated high school and helped to defeat the plan. But its insistence on an integrated Waller was about maintaining whites' position in the neighborhood as much as a commitment to equal opportunity for students of color. At an executive committee meeting in 1964, board members agreed on two reasons to "keep Waller High School bi-racial." First, "because it is right." Second, because "it is essential to the conservation of the community."

"If Waller becomes an all-Negro school it will be difficult to hold present white families or draw new white families," the committee concluded. "The conservation program depends on maintaining a white majority in a bi-racial neighborhood."

In addition to attempting to persuade whites to be more accepting of their Puerto Rican and black neighbors, LPCA did make some efforts to recruit people of color as members, or at least engage them in dialogue. But these efforts had only limited success.

One of the first such outreach efforts followed another backlash to the strict enforcement campaign. In the summer of 1958, LPCA brought the landlord of 477 Deming Pl., an apartment building just a block from the lake north of Old Town, to court. Claiming the building was overcrowded, it asked for the tenants to be evicted until the building's layout could be changed.

The landlord charged LPCA with targeting his building because a number of its tenants were Puerto Rican. Trying to defuse the accusation, LPCA met with representatives of Puerto Rican organizations. Their message was that the tenants' evictions would be for their own good: "We are not against them as a group," a staffer explained, "but are interested in seeing that they live within health and safety standards." But as with other evictions related to the strict enforcement campaign, no alternative housing arrangements had been made for the tenants of 477 Deming Pl. LPCA's representatives also complained that the tenants had made too much noise at night. Unsurprisingly, no long-term relationships appear to have been built from the meeting.

LPCA made a few more proactive efforts in the early 1960s. In 1962, it published "LPCA es para usted" ("LPCA is for you"), a Spanish-language pamphlet that was distributed to recruit Puerto Rican and Latino membership. Two years later, it held a summit with the Puerto Rican Congress, a local advocacy group, that was attended by two dozen people. But most of them were property owners, like LPCA's members, which left out the overwhelming majority of Puerto Ricans in Lincoln Park who rented, and were therefore most vulnerable to the strict enforcement campaign. In any event, LPCA remained an almost exclusively white Anglo organization.

The most consequential move in this period was the formation of an LPCA Human Relations Committee under the leadership of the Rev. James Reed. Reed, who was white, led a congregation at the Church of the Holy Covenant in the neighborhood and had been active in civil rights organizing in Chicago. While his committee was not very successful in recruiting more Puerto Ricans or blacks to LPCA, it would become a caucus agitating for more aggressive anti-displacement policies within the organization—and eventually a base for anti-urban renewal activism.

In the early 1960s, Puerto Ricans and Appalachian whites weren't the only newcomers causing rehabbers some discomfort. LPCA and OTTA also began to confront a new and unexpected challenge: larger private developers. This also marked an important new phase in the evolution of Lincoln Park.

For years, rehabbers had focused on increasing investments wherever they could, both through public coercion (asking courts to force landlords to renovate their properties) and private persuasion (lobbying banks to issue more mortgages). But as the amount of money flowing into the wealthier eastern side of Lincoln Park grew, they increasingly looked to regulate, redirect, or even stop it altogether. It was as if investment were a faucet: The rehabbers had needed to turn it on to fund their own mortgages and renovations, even as poorer residents were sometimes flushed out. But when it became clear that the renovation of Lincoln Park was durable and profitable, the faucet opened even wider and threatened the rehabbers themselves.

Unlike lower-income renters, of course, most middle-class homeowners were not at risk of losing their homes. But as developers and businesses were increasingly attracted to the neighborhood, they threatened to change the "character" the rehabbers held dear. Even as they created a model of what would come to be called gentrification, the rehabbers also popularized a middle class anti-gentrification narrative focused on the physical urban form and notions of historical and cultural authenticity.

One sign of this new investment activity was the changing commercial character of Wells Street. The street had been a relatively quiet, unremarkable strip of half-vacant storefronts stacked under brick apartments throughout the 1940s. In the 1950s, a new bookstore and Dill Pickle-inspired bar began to give Wells the artsy, educated vibe of Old Town's new rehabbers.

The early 1960s saw a new kind of Wells Street: a hip and grungy nightlife spot that drew the rowdy and the curious from all over the Chicago area and beyond. In one eighteen month period in 1962 and 1963, twenty-three new bars opened. Nearly every month drew a big profile of the strip's reputation in a regional or national outlet.

"Those who have known Wells Street for years must now

find it almost unrecognizable," one 1963 *Tribune* story went. "Before the recent upsurge of…the city's latest night-life attraction, there were practically no stores along the declining segment north of North Avenue." But now, antique shops and art galleries were joined with cafes and bars that teemed with people, especially on the weekends. Some of them were young hippies; others "squares" from the suburbs looking to be provoked, in an echo of the "slumming" crazy that hit Tower Town nearly half a century earlier.

Like the Tower Towners forty years before, many Old Towners felt that the increasing commercialization of their neighborhood's main street threatened the kind of neighborhood they had built— except now it was a quiet, family-oriented character that needed to be saved, rather than bohemian experimentation. In 1962, OTTA even considered canceling the Art Fair to keep out tourists, though it had worked tirelessly to use the Art Fair to *bring in* visitors just a few years earlier. "Many of use are reluctant to turn our quiet streets into a tourist attraction for two days," an OTTA newsletter editorial wrote. On the other hand, the prominence of the fair "strengthens our position in the city…. Hundreds of thousands of people know about us by now; people will listen."

OTTA decided to keep the fair that year, though the question came up again in 1963. At a panel discussion in September, 300 people listened to OTTA's Paul Angle and John Callaway, a journalist who had written an article entitled "Will Excess Spoil Old Town?", debate the merits of the neighborhood's new activity centers.

Still, when OTTA's membership was surveyed about the Art Fair two months later, eighty-six percent voted to keep it. Even as it became wealthier, Old Towners treasured their reputation as more culturally sophisticated and freewheeling than other well-to-do neighborhoods. "People who wore coats and ties would live in Near North," one resident said, referring to the area around the Gold Coast. "People who preferred sports shirts would live in Old Town." Whether the reasons were strategic or artistic—or just a reluctance to give up on tradition—OTTA couldn't quite turn its back on the event, or on its status as one of the hottest cultural centers in the city.

The rehabbers were more aggressive, and more successful, in tamping down new investments in *residential* properties. At the very beginning of the decade, a private developer announced plans to build a five-story apartment building in the Triangle—the first new housing construction in Old Town since before the Great Depression.

At first, OTTA celebrated. After all, attracting private investments had been a central goal at the founding of the Triangle Association in 1948. In barely over a decade, their efforts had profoundly changed the local real estate market: renovations had brought blocks formerly shunned by the middle class onto the front page of the *Tribune*'s society pages; certification as an official conservation area had removed the stain of redlining. Between 1950 and 1960, median rents had increased by more than seventy percent.

But the new apartments didn't live up to OTTA's standards in a number of other ways. For one, they were actually *new*, interrupting the Victorian aesthetic the rehabbers cultivated with a "sterile" modern design they associated with anonymous downtown towers. Second, they were *apartments*: relatively high-density, small units, and rented, the opposite in every respect from the large, owner-occupied single family houses that OTTA considered the ideal. And because the units were less than ideal, the Association determined, so would be the people who lived in them.

"High priced slums for transients," was the judgment of an OTTA editorial. "The people of this community—who are this community," it continued, setting aside the fact that most OTTA members were relatively recent transplants themselves, "will be replaced by transients."

Even rehabbing became a fraught activity. Through the 1950s, the vast majority of people who bought a building to renovate in Old Town had been small-timers looking to join the local "creative" community as homeowners and perhaps landlords of another building or two. The very act of renovating had helped them build relationships with other rehabbers. "You find a neighbor who knows how to do things to teach you," one explained. "You end up swapping horror stories, exchanging the names of good plasterers. There's a…bond between people who have suffered this way." Another homeowner's description underlined the extent to which rehabbers, though far wealthier than most other residents of their new neighborhoods, identified as lower-income people bootstrapping their way forward: "Many of [my neighbors] came here first because they couldn't afford property elsewhere and they could substitute their own work for the money they didn't have to achieve the kind of homes they wanted."

This self-identity—struggling creative spirits renovating homes as a kind of communal artistic practice—differed strongly from the perceptions of new corporate developers.

But with banks suddenly willing to lend and land values skyrocketing, professional developers began to enter the market in greater numbers in the early 1960s. And it wasn't just that the people managing the renovations were now increasingly disconnected from those bonds. So were the people they rented to, who came to the neighborhood with different ideas about the kind of community they were paying substantial rents to live in.

"I generally buy on the fringes where it's not so rough that people will not move into it," one developer told a researcher. "I rent to young professionals, and I've found that they can't handle lower class people."

In the wake of these shifts, "strict zoning enforcement" came to have a new meaning for OTTA and LPCA. In addition to forcing existing buildings to change, these groups began to use zoning to fight off new developments—an option that had not been available to the Tower Towners. In particular, they began to argue—mostly with success—for a moratorium on new buildings until the official conservation plan could be finalized and put into place. And by 1964, after almost a decade, that was finally on the verge of happening.

————————————

The first breakthrough in crafting the conservation plan had occurred back in 1960, when LPCA agreed to a compromise with urban renewal authorities. Rather than a quick, comprehensive program that would transform the entire neighborhood at once, Lincoln Park's conservation would proceed in stages, one section of the community at a time, under something called a "General Neighborhood Renewal Plan" (GNRP).

Within a few months of the decision to create a GNRP, the federal government approved Chicago's application for planning funds. Mayor Daley appointed members to the Lincoln Park Conservation Community Council—the official body that would convey local recommendations to the City Council and Washington. There was finally a live federal conservation program under way in Lincoln Park.

The task of writing the GNRP represented a key moment in the evolution of Lincoln Park. With de facto control over the process, the rehabbers faced a number of choices about how to codify their own ideas about what the neighborhood ought to be; how and whether to incorporate the opinions of their neighbors who did not belong to LPCA or its affiliated groups; and how to understand and weigh the tradeoffs between making the neighborhood's appearance and reputation more middle class and maintaining the social diversity they said they valued.

By the early 1960s, the rehabbers had evidence that, at least in Old Town, their campaign to preserve the neighborhood for the middle class—and, ostensibly, everyone else—could be successful. And they had heard some neighbors' concerns that the rehabbers' success was coming at their expense. But though LPCA and its affiliates continued to insist that they would defend against displacement wherever possible, the General Neighborhood Renewal Plan they approved reflected much the same set of priorities and tactics they had been pursuing for a decade—and did so without significant input from other neighborhood residents.

John Cook summarized LPCA's approach in a speech at LPCA's annual membership meeting in January 1961. Cook had moved to Old Town—Crilly Court, in fact—back in 1945, after graduating from the University of Chicago. A practicing lawyer, he helped found both OTTA and LPCA. In 1961, speaking as LPCA's retiring president, he laid out the organization's vision for the next chapter of its work.

Like most rehabbers, Cook believed LPCA's work had importance far beyond Lincoln Park. The conservation program, private and public, was a kind of grand experiment to see "whether the older areas can be preserved and whether the trend to the suburbs can be reversed"; whether the rehabbers could transcend the white middle class' choice between prosperous but sterile suburbs on the one hand, and culturally rich but economically and racially "doomed" cities on the other. If they succeeded, they might have a template to preserve not just Lincoln Park, but Chicago as a whole, and perhaps other American cities, for the white middle classes then moving en masse to the suburbs.

Though Cook pitched conservation as a way to create an alternative to suburban life for the white middle class, in many ways his vision for Lincoln Park borrowed from suburban models. From an urban planning perspective, LPCA's vision of relatively low-density, owner-occupied housing oriented towards nuclear families, and stricter separation of residential and commercial areas, was a quintessentially suburban orientation, even if its starting point was an older, denser, more mixed-use neighborhood.

More subtly, Cook also pushed a suburban attitude towards

governance. For decades, moving across the city limits had not just put distance between middle-class families in the suburbs and aging city neighborhoods. It had meant severing *political* ties as well: not having to share tax revenue, schools, or decision-making power with the people in those neighborhoods. Cook told LPCA's membership that they should demand something similar.

"We are big enough and wealthy enough and interested enough to be a city in our own right," he declared. "We should have the privilege of self-government in the determination of the type of community in which we are to live." Lincoln Park wasn't "entitled to any better treatment" than other city neighborhoods, he said, but its "special situation" meant that it should be "singled out" for exceptional public services—"regardless of budget problems and the stress of needs for other city areas."

And as with suburbs—which often used their powers of self-government to regulate housing and transportation in ways designed to exclude people of color and people with low incomes—Cook imagined Lincoln Park as the kind of community that could screen out people it considered undesirable.

"What this neighborhood needs," he said, "is the enforcement of those standards by which ninety-five percent of us live, rather than the standards of the lowest five percent." And while he reaffirmed LPCA's stance in favor of civil rights, he also warned that "it is just as essential that the rights of all of us be protected against lawlessness from any minority of the community."

In practice, Cook said, this meant that "people must be removed from dangerous, dilapidated, or overcrowding buildings." The federal conservation program could be used as a more powerful branch of the "strict enforcement" campaign, with its funds for seizing and demolishing "substandard" homes.

To some extent, many of these measures could be justified on public health grounds. But Cook made clear that getting rid of the people who lived in "dangerous" buildings was a goal in itself. For example, he suggested that one way to "eliminate the use of buildings for marginal roomers" would be to ban overnight on-street parking. Lincoln Park residents would then have to choose between paying for a space in a private lot or moving out of the neighborhood. "I do not believe [rooming house residents] would pay to park their cars," he concluded, "and many would find lodging elsewhere." Once again, the noble task of improving unsafe living conditions was paired with actions that suggested the aim was removing the people who lived in buildings deemed unsafe, as much as the buildings themselves.

Throughout 1961, LPCA also solicited input from the seven neighborhood organizations that operated under its umbrella. These groups, for the most part, echoed Cook's address.

In a formal letter outlining its position, the Old Town Triangle Association reiterated longstanding LPCA values, insisting that the neighborhood's "private renewal" depended on "the inherent values of a low density, family residential neighborhood in close proximity to the center of a great city." Its new residents, "pioneers of the old...with a strong feeling for life in surroundings suggesting post-Victorian graciousness," came to get away from both "new apartment buildings and suburbs." The fact that those were the named alternatives, of course, suggested that OTTA had a very specific economic and racial demographic in mind—one that did not include, for instance, the scores of new Lincoln Park residents whose homes had been demolished to construct Sandburg Village.

Its concrete requests mirrored these values: No large new buildings, and no further demolition within the Triangle. OTTA also suggested protecting its quiet by redesigning the street grid, directing cars away from the interior residential areas. Ogden Avenue, a major thoroughfare that ran from Old Town's western edge southwest towards the Cabrini-Green public housing project, would be closed, replaced with a mix of low-rise residential development and pedestrian paths. North Avenue, on the other hand—the dense commercial strip that formed a racial boundary with the area to the south—would be razed and widened into a "modified expressway."

The Lincoln Central Association, representing the area just to the west and north of Old Town, also wanted conservation with a light touch, retaining the area's "essential charm and character" without too much demolition. But it was also conscious of the who, not just the what, of conservation. It suggested a continued focus on deconverting smaller apartments and eliminating rooming houses, while encouraging the arrival "responsible, permanent residents." And it endorsed a tentative plan to tear down nearly every building on Larrabee Street, a low-rent strip of apartments, stores, bars, and garages just west of Old Town—as well as the elimination of two densely packed blocks of apartments at the heart of the Puerto Rican area to create a park.

The Mid-North Association, which had founded LPCA with the OTTA back in 1954, wrote that conservation should embrace the "exchange and diversity of the city," and "reject the distance and isolation of the suburbs." But it, too, asked to use zoning laws to keep "living units to a reasonably large size" and "return as closely as possible to the pattern established when this community was built: Two and three-story houses, with not more than one living unit per floor wherever possible." The Mid-North Association did not specify what would happen to the thousands of households and families who would need to be removed to make that vision a reality.

The planned demolitions on Larrabee Street and North Avenue would not only disproportionately affect lower-income Lincoln Parkers. Laid over a map of the neighborhood's demographics, they also clearly corresponded to the boundaries between Lincoln Park's wealthier, whiter, rehabbed areas, and the increasingly low-income, Latino, and black areas nearby. If Sandburg Village had established a line of segregation between the Gold Coast and poorer areas to the west, it seemed that Lincoln Park's conservation program would do the same for the eastern side of its community.

––––––––––––––––

The planning process highlighted the odd role that LPCA and its affiliates played in Lincoln Park, which blurred formal and informal power, "grassroots" leadership and local democracy. As a private organization whose membership amounted to barely one percent of Lincoln Park's population, LPCA had no official governmental powers—yet it dominated the initial planning of the GNRP. Mayor Daley's appointments to the public body that *did* have official power—the Lincoln Park Conservation Community Council—followed LPCA's recommendations precisely. In fact, every member of the Council was also a member of LPCA. The first Council president, Lyle Mayer, had previously been the president of one of LPCA's neighborhood groups.

For the rehabbers, this was a natural and just situation. After all, who better to lead the conservation program than the local residents who had organized to bring it to the neighborhood? But LPCA's claim to be an authentic representation of the community was flimsy: Its membership made up only a small portion of the area's residents, and overwhelmingly excluded poorer, older, renting, southern, Latino, and black Lincoln Parkers. Those who felt excluded by LPCA's "grassroots" leadership challenged the organization's legitimacy in particular instances, as in the strict enforcement campaign. They also raised their voices about conservation. A June 1960 newsletter column puzzled that, "contrary to one's expectations, the announcement [of the GNRP] apparently has raised some fears."

But in the early 1960s, the rehabbers did not yet face a strong, organized opposition. So it was not a surprise that the plan approved by the Community Council in May of 1962 was very similar to the one LPCA's board had passed a few months earlier. The City Council, in turn, quickly voted to send the 125-page report to Washington for final review. In February 1963, federal urban renewal officials formally accepted Lincoln Park's GNRP.

In addition to zoning and building code guidelines, traffic circulation patterns, and paeans to the neighborhood's "charm and distinction," the GNRP laid out the borders that had been negotiated for the first phase of renewal, called "Project One." Eager to take advantage of federal funds and wary of more delays, many stakeholders—including powerful and resourced institutions like DePaul University—had lobbied to be included in Project One. But in the end, DePaul and most of the rest of Lincoln Park was left out. Of LPCA's seven neighborhood groups, only one managed to get its entire territory included: the Old Town Triangle Association. From the Triangle, the borders stretched a few blocks north, into the Mid-North Association, and west, into the Lincoln Central Association, with a small panhandle over the heart of the Puerto Rican community around Armitage and Halsted.

With the GNRP approved, LPCA—working through the official Community Council—began planning Project One in earnest.

But even as the rehabbers prepared to wield the immense power of federal resources for the first time, they quickly discovered that there were costs as well. Since 1954, LPCA had been accountable only to its overwhelmingly white, professional members. The Community Council, on the other hand, faced federal requirements to hold public hearings, and it did—dozens of them. At these hearings, for the first time, Lincoln Parkers who didn't belong to LPCA had an opportunity to formally, and publicly, weigh in on the changes that had been occurring in the neighborhood for over a decade, and those that were planned for the next decade. It was these hearings which marked the inauguration of the "battle" that LPCA had light-heartedly predicted just a few years earlier.

PART THREE

THE BATTLE OF LINCOLN PARK

1964-1971

CHAPTER 5
PROJECT ONE

The battle of Lincoln Park was a bitter, sometimes violent fight over the future of the community. While the target of unrest was always the same—LPCA, the rehabbers, and government urban renewal agencies—several different groups emerged to challenge them over the rest of the 1960s. Each carried its own distinct, though often overlapping, reasons and strategies for opposing LPCA's agenda. The first phase of battle was carried forward by people whose homes were to be directly demolished by Project One of the conservation program. The next challenge emerged largely from within LPCA itself, as liberal rehabbers sought to live up to their own ideals about protecting vulnerable people. Finally, the most radical members of LPCA joined with a coalition of radical young Puerto Ricans and others to fight for fundamental shifts in the balance of power in Lincoln Park.

In each case, these Lincoln Parkers challenged the rehabbers' vision about what a good neighborhood looked like—and their narrative about the heroic role they were playing in the restoration of the community. By the end of the decade, they would have convinced a great number of people that neighborhood conservation was the story's villain.

———————————

In February 1964, the Chicago Department of Urban Renewal, LPCA, OTTA, and other rehabber neighborhood organizations began presenting the first draft of Project One to the public at locations around Lincoln Park.

In its introduction, Project One reaffirmed the rehabbers' vision of a prosperous neighborhood that could be physically renovated without resorting to mass demolition or displacement. It promised to preserve both the nineteenth century charm of the area's historic building stock and the distinctive class diversity of its residents.

But once the presenters began to explain Project One's specific provisions, their neighbors might have wondered whether they were speaking about the same document. It proposed demolishing 2,100 homes in 644 buildings, or nearly one out of every three in the Project One area—a level of physical destruction unheard of in Old Town since the Great Fire of 1871.

The implications for the neighborhood's class diversity were nearly as dire as for its buildings. The vast majority of demolition was concentrated in the west, far from the rehabber strongholds along the lakefront, where the neighborhood's lower-income residents would be most hard hit. Two streets in particular— Larrabee on the west and North Avenue on the south—would be almost entirely cleared. A third major demolition area covered two blocks with a relatively high Puerto Rican population near Halsted and Armitage, which were to be replaced by a park. Moreover, according to the official conservation survey, nearly half of the buildings planned for demolition were neither "dilapidated" nor "in an advanced state of deterioration," and would be eliminated simply to provide a clean slate for redevelopment, calling to mind slum clearance projects like Lake Meadows in Bronzeville that the rehabbers claimed to reject.

The Project One draft hastened to add that it would be "essential to replace a significant percentage" of the buildings demolished at "a cross section of…income levels." To do so, there would be four sites for low-income public housing, and several for moderate-income housing under a federal program called 221d(3).

But as the phrase "significant percentage" implied, these homes would not match the number to be torn down—nor would they come close. Moreover, the plan made no provision for the rapidly growing number of people being priced out by private rehabilitation, which it hoped to accelerate. A survey conducted for the GNRP found that privately renovated apartments in Lincoln Park increased their rents by an average of eighty percent. Project One proposed to upgrade nearly all unrenovated, "substandard" housing—avoided by the middle class either because it was too cramped and shabby, or because of genuine safety issues—without any steps to cushion the blow on lower-income renters.

These shortfalls did not go unnoticed. As rehabbers and renewal officials took their plans to community meetings, their presentations quickly became tense, particularly near areas slated for demolition. In March, the director of Chicago's Department of Urban Renewal, Lewis Hill, came to a meeting near Larrabee Street. He was met with "a barrage of questions and accusations, some not voiced in moderate tones." Some attendees simply worried about where they would go when their homes were taken. Others had more structural criticisms.

"If the plan is just for the middle class," one woman told Hill, "you are destroying the varied neighborhood you say you want."

In several areas, residents began organizing to stop Project One. Many of these organizers, like the rehabbers to the east, were property owners who had invested significant time and money into their buildings. Unlike most of the rehabbers, however, they were often older longtime residents.

One group formed in the two-block area slated for a new park. Led by people like William Grimmich, who had owned a building on Shakespeare Street for thirty-eight years, and Yvonne Newlin, whose family had invested $30,000 in a nearby building they had owned for twenty-five years, the group passed out flyers and petitioned elected officials on behalf of the four hundred families who would be displaced.

"Where will they go?" Grimmich asked a reporter, bringing up the specter of earlier renewal demolitions. "The people who get displaced won't be able to afford rents in fancy places such as Sandburg Village."

Another, older group mobilized along the southern border of the Project One area. The North Avenue Business Men's Association represented the small businesses that would be displaced for the widening of North Avenue into a "modified expressway." Speaking for "the barber, the clothier, the grower, the dentist, the lawyer," the Association decried the loss of untold thousands of dollars that business owners had invested into the street.

But the strongest opposition came from Larrabee Street, where nearly every home and business for three-quarters of a mile was to be destroyed. Within days of the release of the first draft of Project One, a group of business owners, landlords, and tenants formed the Larrabee Street Improvement Association.

Like La Clark between the Gold Coast and the Near North Side a decade earlier, Larrabee Street represented a kind of border between the increasingly affluent Old Town to the east, and the increasingly poor, and black, southwest corner of Lincoln Park to the west. Its storefronts held a mix of bars, garages, and corner stores; above them were apartments home to longtime white residents, blacks, Puerto Ricans, and young artists who could no longer afford to live in Old Town.

"This plan was formulated without consulting us, and without regard for our interests or our fate…and so we are determined to resist the cold, impersonal force behind [it]," wrote one member of the Larrabee Street Improvement Association. "There is no reason why the Lincoln Park community should exclude people like us or streets like ours."

Though urban renewal may have seemed like an "impersonal force" to many of the organizers, it was their neighbors who met at the next LPCA meeting in April 1964 to decide whether to formally endorse the Project One draft and recommend approval by the official Community Council and Department of Urban Renewal. On the day of the meeting, LPCA members were joined by residents from Larrabee Street and other designated clearance areas, who came to implore their fellow Lincoln Parkers not to tear down their homes.

One woman, from the area of the proposed park, arrived with a simple sign she held up facing the crowd: "Save Your Homes—Down With Urban Renewal." Others shouted angry protests. Many others delivered testimony or wrote letters.

"Nothing ever got conserved with a bulldozer," wrote one couple who lived above the convenience store they had owned for thirty-six years. "For whom is the street to be conserved? If not for the people who live on it then it is a matter of open discrimination. If you clear it as was done on LaSalle Street, and build what was built on LaSalle Street [Sandburg Village], then the street has not been renewed, but replaced.... What has really happened is that you have destroyed our home and replaced us with another more affluent group of people whom you feel deserve the convenience of what was once ours more than we do."

Others insisted that if LPCA called off the wrecking balls, they would be able to bring their homes up to the rehabbers' standards on their own. "We are aware that our street has begun to deteriorate," wrote a resident of Larrabee. "We are equally sure that it is in our power to preserve it."

At least one LPCA board member joined to issue his own rebuke. The Rev. Alva Tompkins had lived two blocks west of Larrabee since 1942, and now felt "outraged" on behalf of his neighbors.

Tompkins told the story of a sixty-seven-year-old woman who had just bought her home after working for thirty years as a secretary, and would now have it torn down. "By what right," he asked his fellow LPCA members, "do we evict homeowners and tenants from their homes? ...Is she going to be treated as the government has treated the Seneca Indians?"

Project One set off by far the largest, most sustained opposition to LPCA up to that point. But by then, LPCA had evicted hundreds of residents through the strict enforcement campaign, not to mention many others removed when rehabbers purchased apartments to renovate or convert to single-family homes. What made this time different?

One factor may have been the concentrated nature of the demolitions and evictions proposed under Project One. In the strict enforcement campaign, buildings were targeted one at a time; an owner and their tenants taken to court would usually be the only ones in the immediate vicinity. Project One, on the other hand, plotted the demolition of entire blocks, or even entire streets. That meant lots of natural allies among neighbors, some of whom may have known each other for years and had relationships they could build into organizations.

Second, Project One carried a very different decision-making structure than previous changes that LPCA had pursued. Before Project One, those changes been the result of many small decisions, each of which was made by someone unlikely to be swayed by public protest. The judges who presided over the court cases that emerged from the strict enforcement campaign were at least supposed to be working from objective standards about whether buildings did or did not meet the city's codes. And the hundreds of rehabbers who bought and remodeled homes were private citizens, accountable only to their own desires and finances.

Under Project One, however, the entire plan—the fate of hundreds of buildings and thousands of people—could be blocked, or amended, by a single vote of any number of public bodies: the Community Council, the Department of Urban Renewal, or the City Council.

LPCA had asked for a federal conservation program in order to transform their dispersed, private efforts into a consolidated plan backed by government resources. But the rehabbers' earlier scattershot efforts had meant scattered enemies, fragmented and weak. The very powers they fought for and won—the ability to make sweeping decisions to transform entire swaths of the neighborhood once—also created a larger, more united group of people with reason to join together to stop them.

———————————

Despite this unity, these opponents did not convince enough LPCA members to vote down the Project One draft at the April 1964 meeting. But they did succeed in setting off a tense debate within the Association.

On one side, some members dismissed the protests as selfish. "There are people…who have not participate[d] in the hard work of seriously considering what is best for our entire community," a homeowner in Lincoln Central wrote the LPCA board, "and who now suddenly purport to 'represent' the common people."

Others accused the protesters of threatening their investments. "Many people have improved their property at great expense because they were led to believe that urban assistance was coming," wrote Kathryn Jay Rodington, who owned a building on Clark Street. "We are not…safe from invasion by slum conditions and slum dwellers. Take away the proposal and vast areas of the Lincoln Park community will slip in value."

On the other side were people like the Rev. Alva Tompkins and Rev. James Reed, head of LPCA's Human Relations Committee, who condemned the displacement in stark moral terms.

But most of the rehabbers seemed to settle in between: sympathetic to those about to lose their homes, yet convinced that conservation had to be carried out. This middle position was less a compromise, however, than a refusal to acknowledge that some of their asserted priorities were becoming increasingly incompatible with each other.

The rehabbers staking out a middle ground offered expressions of deep concern for those who would be displaced and a commitment to preserve the neighborhood's diversity. The OTTA released a statement underlining that the "purpose of Urban Renewal should be…to permit a multiversity of residents—of all ages and at all income levels, such as live in the area now." The Mid-North Association requested that "all possible effort be made to provide living space for people displaced by the GNRP within the area of Project One."

The centrists proposed a number of specific measures to reach these goals. On North Avenue, they asked that evicted merchants be given priority leases in the planned new shopping center. And they supported the construction of income-restricted housing "to help retain as many of the present residents as possible…and maintain Lincoln Park as a community in which people of varying financial means may live as good neighbors."

But there was little reckoning with the fact that the number of people displaced would inevitably far outstrip the amount of new housing available to them—or that many people would be evicted before any of the new income-restricted homes had been built. And the most obvious way to retain as many residents as possible—not carrying out large-scale demolition of their homes—was never seriously considered.

More fundamentally, the rehabbers failed, or refused, to grasp the consequences of their own success. Their goals—more middle-class families, higher-quality housing, and increasing property values—had been formed when it seemed that Lincoln Park's greatest threat was economic deprivation. But on the neighborhood's eastern edge, middle-class homeowners no longer existed in small enclaves. The Old Town Triangle had changed, but the goals had not changed.

Even as they expressed concerns about losing the neighborhood's diversity, LPCA marked its tenth anniversary by uncritically celebrating the acceleration of private rehabilitation. A "home improvement show" invited Chicagoans to tour recently renovated homes, such as a twenty-eight-unit rooming house that now housed a single family.

At an anniversary gala in September attended by Mayor Daley, a speaker bragged that such renovation activity had increased even more since the beginning of the GNRP process. From 1958 through 1961, Lincoln Park had averaged $445,000 of renovation activity a year. But after the start of the GNRP process, there had been $904,000 in 1962, $1.23 million in 1963—and $1.22 million in just the first eight months of 1964.

William Hutchison, who had moved to Old Town back in 1936 during the heydey of the Carl Street studios, told the gala crowd, "We are attempting to retain all that was good in the past." But LPCA could not reconcile its members' conviction that while the diversity low-income residents provided was "good," the kinds of housing that allowed those residents to remain in the neighborhood were not.

This refusal to follow through on stated contradictions expressed itself in many ways. One was a general opposition to the amount and kinds of new low-income housing that might actually offset Project One clearance. A prominent couple in Old Town warned that "public housing becomes one the biggest detriments to securing…private financing" that middle-class residents depended on for their purchases and renovations. And when plans were made for public housing, the rehabbers' commitment to large homes and families suddenly flipped. Project One called for 256 homes in public housing, but of those, just sixteen were for families. The other 238 were small apartments restricted to the elderly. This reversal carried significant racial overtones: By that time, residents of family public housing were nearly entirely black, while half of the tenants in public housing for the elderly were still white.

The continued drive to orient the neighborhood towards middle-class homeowners in large houses also shaped the rehabbers' attitudes towards new private housing. OTTA asked the city to enact low-density zoning laws that would block new apartment buildings that targeted younger renters with smaller units. These studios and one-bedroom apartments were more expensive than unrenovated older buildings, but much cheaper than the houses and large apartments preferred by the rehabbers. "The building would indeed fill up with persons," OTTA's board wrote about one such proposal. "But not with our residents." Again, types of housing were judged primarily by the kinds of people they were perceived to attract, or permit, to live in the neighborhood.

Rehabbers often justified these policies with references to housing quality and safety. But when asked to directly choose between priorities, the results could be revealing. In one case, a group of homeowners informed a nearby landlord that, according to city code, his building had too few fire escapes to serve the number of apartments. When he announced plans to build a new fire escape, however, five dozen neighbors joined with LPCA to object because the unsightly structure might "devalue their property." Instead, LPCA's executive director suggested, the landlord should deconvert from six to three units— evicting half the tenants—to avoid the need for a front fire escape at all.

With LPCA's stamp of approval, the Project One plan moved on to official votes by the Lincoln Park Conservation Community Council and the City Council in the summer of 1965. These sparked a flurry of new protests. The Larrabee Street Improvement Association brought 200 people to a public hearing by the Community Council—but, before they had time to speak, the Council announced that time for comment had run out.

Instead, Larrabee Street residents sent a bundle of letters to the City Council containing the testimony they had intended to deliver. They began with a protest that their time had been taken up with speakers lined up in favor of Project One, such as DePaul University Vice President Father Theodore Wangler, who promised the crowd that "people will not suffer too much."

"What is too much?" Larrabee Street Improvement Association president Harley Budd asked. "This attitude is not usually associated with the ministry."

Budd also attacked the legitimacy of LPCA as a community organization, pointing out that its membership made up only a small fraction of the total Lincoln Park population. "Why should forty percent of the residents of an area," Budd asked, "be the victims of the whim of less than one percent?"

Several writers noted that Larrabee Street provided a kind of housing opportunity they wouldn't find elsewhere. An elderly black couple, E. and Lorene Gomillia, praised the neighborhood's relative acceptance of racial integration. "We cannot understand how a neighborhood like this could be torn out when every newspaper in the country is filled every day with talk of discrimination," they wrote.

The Gomillias also promised that they would be able to bring the street up to the rehabbers' standards without clearance. "We think Larrabee Street is probably one of the best streets in the United States," they added. "We know it may not look real modern, but if Urban Renewal will leave us alone we will all fix our own buildings."

Like many other residents of Larrabee Street, the Gomillias had already been displaced by a previous urban renewal project, the Cabrini-Green development. Others, especially southern whites and Puerto Ricans, had been moved by clearance for Sandburg Village. The Gomillias were not alone, then, in their despair that if they were evicted from Larrabee, it would not be the last time: "There is no place else for us to go that the same thing will not happen to us again."

Once again, the protesters went unheeded. The Community Council and City Council approved Project One despite the protests.

That left federal approval as the last hurdle. Larrabee Street residents flyered and organized heavily to bring residents to the last public hearing in November. Their literature abandoned the cajoling, pleading, or rationalizing tones of earlier testimony for open militancy: "All wars are fought for the ownership of land…. Should our American be blood be spread all over the world to save land for others, and our own land be taken from one American and given to another American just because the one has more money and political power than the other?" To residents, it promised war: "Your presence [at the hearing] will be the same as a gun on the battle front."

But the Larrabee Street Improvement Association was not able to convince Washington officials to override the plan their wealthier neighbors had endorsed. Project One received final approval in December 1965, with clearance scheduled to begin the following spring.

During this first phase of resistance, LPCA members who

sympathized with the protesters worked primarily to try to bring more dissenting voices within LPCA.

One of the leaders of this outreach was Rev. James Reed. Reed was something of a dissenter himself, often initiating conversations about race, poverty, and displacement on the Association's board. Yet his attempts to bring in like-minded neighbors from outside the Association were often less than successful. Reed organized Spanish-language meetings and forums on behalf of LPCA, but complained that they attracted few attendees. LPCA also printed another round of Spanish-language brochures, but little came of them.

In December 1965, an LPCA staffer named Luis Cuza helped create a more permanent outreach infrastructure in the Spanish American Federation. A coalition of Hispanic businesses and community organizations, the Federation worked closely with LPCA on housing and jobs issues. In April, the Spanish American Federation, LPCA, and a progressive religious group called the North Side Cooperative Ministry joined to form the Lincoln Park Redevelopment Corporation, which aimed to build limited-income replacement housing in the Project One area.

In the midst of this work, the bulldozers arrived. Around the time the the Spanish American Federation held its first meeting in January 1966, the city's Department of Urban Renewal purchased its first property under Project One on Ogden Avenue at the edge of the Old Town Triangle. In April, an old hospital building became the first to be razed.

Project One proceeded slowly for most of 1966. After the first six months of the year, less than five percent of the total planned displacement had taken place. Still, the beginning of actual evictions under Project One led to new appeals for LPCA to reconsider its tactics and goals. An indication of the extent to which the last two years had widened the debate appeared in the March issue of LPCA's newsletter.

In an essay that took up nearly a full page, a Unitarian

Universalist minister named Neil Shadle questioned where urban renewal was taking the neighborhood. Shadle asked Lincoln Parkers whether they wanted to "build a new, unified, and human city for all of Chicago's people" or allow urban renewal to "improve out" the poor. "As it renews itself," he wrote, the "tendency [is] for a community to become more expensive and less diverse." Shadle's challenge to his fellow LPCA members signaled a growing divide within the organization over what "conservation" should look like, and one that would only become more pronounced as Lincoln Park entered the next step in the GNRP.

CHAPTER 6
CONCERNED CITIZENS

With Project One well underway, city officials and rehabbers began planning for Phase Two of Lincoln Park's conservation program—which covered the rest of the GNRP area west to the river and north past the campus of DePaul University—in the atmosphere of debate and agitation that Project One had provoked. (An LPCA newsletter explained that the more neutral "Phase" was meant to replace the growing negative connotations around "Project.")

Affordable housing remained a key flash point within LPCA. James Reed led the charge to include low-income housing in the list of priority policies the group was preparing to send to the Department of Urban Renewal. An initial LPCA board vote approved of Reed's plank; but when the final document was published, it had been deleted.

In fact, LPCA's Phase Two priorities differed little from Project One, applying the same principles to more of Lincoln Park. They called for upgrading schools and commercial districts, but also stepping up the rehabilitation of older, cheaper buildings without proportional measures to blunt the effect on their low-income tenants. And once again, significant areas were suggested for demolition: eight blocks over half a mile along North Avenue west of Larrabee, in one of the poorest sections of Lincoln Park with the highest concentration of black tenants.

The anti-displacement wing of LPCA was furious. "The board speaks for the middle class residents of the area," Reed told the *Chicago Tribune*, pointing out that there were no black, Latino, or Appalachian board members. "They are fighting for themselves."

The next month, Reed and his allies organized Concerned Citizens of Lincoln Park, a caucus within LPCA to call for more low-income housing and minimal displacement. Joining with Spanish American Federation president Sergio Herrera, Concerned Citizens brought public pressure on LPCA to add affordable housing back into its priorities list and attempted to organize new block groups in affected areas.

Reed made this demand at LPCA's December 1966 board meeting. Outside LPCA's offices, Concerned Citizens and the Spanish American Federation brought more than sixty people to picket. Inside, board members debated the resolution.

Reed and Herrera's preferred language called for the "maximum number of low and moderate income" homes to be built, but after a number of revisions, the board moved to vote on an amended resolution that called for "adequate housing for all residents of Lincoln Park." On a 16-14 vote, it passed.

It was a compromise, but Concerned Citizens believed it was a step in the right direction. "The board has responded to a need," Reed told the *Tribune* afterwards. "We feel it was a victory."

———————

For a brief moment, it looked like the December vote marked a turning point that would propel the Concerned Citizens faction to leadership of the rehabbers' movement in Lincoln Park. In January 1967, the LPCA's Nominating Committee released its endorsements for the Board of Directors election to be held later that month. Among the names: Reed and Ramon Campos, a member of both LPCA's Human Relations Committee and the Spanish American Federation who had helped to organize the public campaign around Phase Two affordable housing.

Until 1967, an endorsement by the Nominating Committee had been nearly as good as an win. Though the final decision was officially up to the members, their votes were so reliable that elections for most posts were rarely even contested.

But the fights over housing and displacement had galvanized LPCA's conservative wing as well as those Reed and Campos sought to lead. No sooner had their endorsements been made public than a campaign began to defeat them.

Most of those who opposed Reed and Campos were quick to endorse "diversity" themselves. Rather than focusing on the details of displacement policy, they argued that people who had spent the last several months criticizing LPCA to the press were unfit to lead it. "Quite apart from…Reed's views," wrote twenty-five prominent Lincoln Park residents in a letter that went out to the entire Association's membership, "we do not feel that it makes sense to elect as a director a man who will publicly attack LPCA."

When they did mention housing, the criticism was oblique. The letter said that while LPCA had already "fully recognized" the "necessity" of low-income housing, the Concerned Citizens faction wanted to give it "absolute priority over improved schools and every other important community goal."

If organized opposition to Nominating Committee candidates was a new development, so was the campaign's strategy. LPCA had long allowed members who wished to vote in annual elections but who were sick or out of town to sign a "proxy" vote that could be delivered in their place. But in the lead-up to the 1967 election, the conservatives began collecting as many proxy votes as they could against Reed and Campos. Since relatively few people showed up to vote in person, proxies could swamp the turnout of regular members inclined to support the officially endorsed candidates.

The plan worked. On January 23, at LPCA's annual meeting, Reed and Campos were both soundly defeated.

His supporters cried foul. "I have been shocked and deeply disappointed by reports that...LPCA members have been collecting proxy votes to keep Jim Reed from being elected," said Larry Dutenhaver, who had been nominated for a position as Vice President. "[Proxies were] never intended as an instrument by which a minority could control the annual meeting."

But more than a procedural disagreement, the successful campaign against Reed and Campos added to LPCA's growing crisis of legitimacy as a truly representative community organization. "The issue tonight has become whether the LPCA can continue to be the leading spokesman for the people of Lincoln Park," Dutenhaver charged. "More and more people believe that it does not."

Rev. Sergio Herrera was more specific. "[The poor] are still out there," he warned the crowd after the vote, "even though you have defeated another person genuinely concerned with their wellbeing."

———————————

During the fight over the Project One draft in 1964 and 1965, the harshest criticism of LPCA had come from outside organizations like the Larrabee Street Improvement Association. But in 1966 and 1967, even as more and more people came to publicly question LPCA's legitimacy as a community organization, most anti-displacement leaders would focus on lobbying for change within the Association, rather than challenging it from the outside.

There were probably several reasons for this shift. Perhaps the most important was simply that the first battle was over, and

Larrabee Street residents had lost. The government had officially decided to seize and demolish their homes under Project One. Unlike Reed, Herrera, Campos, Dutenhaver, and others, who did not face eviction from their own homes but opposed displacement on principle, the Larrabee Street Improvement Association had been led by the people who stood to be removed by urban renewal. By 1967, not only had Project One been finalized, but hundreds of Larrabee Street residents had actually been evicted, and most of those no longer remained in Lincoln Park.

Second, for people like Reed and Campos, LPCA and its members remained their most plausible base. They, and most of their allies, belonged to LPCA or to affiliated organizations like the Spanish American Federation. Efforts by Reed and the Human Relations Committee to build more support among the people who might have been their base—the mostly lower-income people most at risk of displacement—had not been successful.

Finally, organizers focused on persuading LPCA leadership simply because LPCA still held more power over urban renewal decisions in Lincoln Park than anyone else. Its reports set the agenda for planning. Its members staffed the Community Council and approved official recommendations for the Department of Urban Renewal and the City Council. Appeals from other organizations during the Project One planning process had mostly been brushed off. If you wanted to change the course of urban renewal, it seemed obvious that you needed to change the conversation within LPCA.

After its losses, Concerned Citizens regrouped to formulate a strategy. That work culminated in April, when it published its demands in a pamphlet called "Renewal or Replacement."

If anything, "Renewal or Replacement" sharpened the charges Reed and others had leveled against LPCA during the leadup to the December board vote. Lincoln Park's conservation program had become "a crisis" for the poorest third of the community, it charged. The "cultural, racial, and economic diversity which gives

Lincoln Park its identity" was at risk. And LPCA was to blame, its efforts on affordable housing limited to "lip service and tokenism."

If Lincoln Park were to be "truly renewed," and not simply "replaced," two things had to happen according to Concerned Citizens. First, all demolitions as part of the conservation program had to be brought to an immediate halt until affordable housing was built on the already-cleared land.

But Concerned Citizens believed that these and other necessary changes would never happen if LPCA continued to represent mostly white middle-class homeowners. So their second demand was that LPCA depose its "self-perpetuating elite" and "[ensure] the widest possible participation...by all segments of the community." Specifically, they called for reducing membership fees from the established $10, or $5 for renters; holding board meetings "at times when working people can attend"; making more meetings open to all members, rather than just the Board of Directors; and abolishing the Nominating Committee to allow for openly contested elections of all board members.

Though in some ways a broadside against LPCA, "Renewal or Replacement" nevertheless ended up calling for *more* power to be concentrated in the Association. Once LPCA had been made more representative, the pamphlet argued that the Community Council ought to be formally brought under its control. "As a democratic association of residents, [LPCA] ought to and can become the structure through which the voice of the community is heard."

In this sense, Concerned Citizens' manifesto was profoundly optimistic. The problem, it argued, was not so much with what some Lincoln Parkers wanted, but "the authoritarian whimsy of self-serving bureaucrats, politicians, and housing profiteers." If only Lincoln Park residents could "establish the control over our own affairs" they could "bring the benefits of community renewal [to] the community."

LPCA's response, published as a letter from the president in the May newsletter, highlighted past accommodations and dismissed most future changes. On the one hand, it promised to allow internal debate on the proposals around elections and said that meeting times had already been moved to after-work hours. On the other, it rejected lower membership dues as impossible, and questioned whether "Renewal or Replacement" was meant to be constructive criticism, or simply slander against LPCA.

But the true distance between Concerned Citizens and LPCA was greater than this exchange revealed. Both sides believed they were arguing over how best to "bring the benefits of community renewal [to] the community." But they did not agree on who, exactly, was a legitimate member of the community.

Perhaps more than LPCA, Concerned Citizens believed that "the community" was simply the people who actually lived in Lincoln Park. But their definition was also shaped by their ideals of what kind of neighborhood Lincoln Park ought to be. Though "Renewal or Replacement" claimed that "racial diversity" was core to Lincoln Park's identity, the area had in fact been nearly all-white until recently, and the eastern side still was. When Puerto Rican, black, and Appalachian migrants settled in the central and western side of the neighborhood in the 1950s, they had scarcely had time to move in before coming under threat from rising rents and government bulldozers. People like Reed and Campos were trying to build a new, inclusive version of Lincoln Park as much as defend an existing one.

LPCA, for its part, had always defined "community" in large part in terms of personal characteristics. When former Executive Director William Friedlander wrote back in 1962 that "Personal standards, and not ethnic background, are the basis of acceptance in the community," he meant to emphasize "not ethnic background" for white LPCA members nervous about integration. But he was also affirming that the Association would not accept Lincoln

Parkers whose "standards" it disapproved of. Belonging, and earning a voice in community decisions, was about contributing in ways that the rehabbers found valuable. The highest form of contribution, of course, was to own and tastefully renovate one or more homes. Cultural contributions were important, too, whether that meant paintings at the Old Town art fair or institutions that enhanced the area's diversity, such as the Buddhist temple.

But people who failed to make these kind of contributions— or, worse, who found fault with them, like those who protested the strict enforcement campaign—did not belong. To many rehabbers, it was self-evident that people they called "transients," from lower-income renters whose music was too loud to higher-income renters unwilling or unable to purchase a home and join LPCA, were not productive members of the community—and therefore did not have a right to live in Lincoln Park.

———————

Aside from the occasional newsletter item celebrating an eviction of low-income renters, LPCA had generally downplayed the harsher implications of their beliefs, even internally. Since its first public statement of non-discrimination in 1958, the Association had emphasized both ethnic and economic inclusion. And the celebration of diversity as a positive feature of the community went back at least to the Old Town Triangle Association in the 1940s.

But in 1967, signs appeared that some rehabbers were ready to rethink that rhetoric. In a sense, they were confronting the tensions that had always existed between their ideas about an "improved" community and the effect those improvements had on lower-income people. While Reed, Campos, and their allies acknowledged that tension and came down on the side of expanding conservation to accommodate diversity, now some people began to suggest that diversity might have to be sacrificed to conservation.

A few months after LPCA president Roland Whitman used his newsletter column to respond to "Renewal or Replacement," he used it to suggest Lincoln Parkers read a different urban renewal pamphlet: a reflection on the program in Hyde Park by Muriel Beadle, the wife of the Chancellor of the University of Chicago.

According to Beadle, Whitman explained, Hyde Park had successfully managed racial integration. But it had done so by establishing the neighborhood as a center of *middle-class* integration. Keeping out all black Chicagoans was impossible, given Hyde Park's location in the heart of the South Side. But slum clearance could remove low-income people—and by removing people who threatened Hyde Park's middle-class identity, middle-class flight to the suburbs could be avoided. "The bitterest pill that the community had to swallow," Beadle wrote, "was to accept the fact that the stated objectives of conservation and renewal could not be obtained unless (1) the community accepted integration; (2) treated integration as a class problem; and (3) discriminated against lower-income families and individuals." She explained further: "Urban renewal has not left [Hyde Park-Kenwood] economically integrated, because of demolition and rehabilitation which necessarily displaced low-income families.... [Y]ou can't have a middle-class residential community unless the majority of the people who live in it have middle-class incomes." Copies of the booklet, Whitman advised, were available at the LPCA office.

There were other indications that LPCA's leadership was moving to be less sympathetic to the anti-displacement cause even as Concerned Citizens became more strident in their advocacy. Most seriously, six months after maneuvering to keep Rev. Reed from the LPCA Board of Directors, the Association's leadership removed him from his longtime post as chairman of the Human Relations Committee. (The new chairman would not bother to hold a meeting for the rest of the year.) And when the Nominating Committee met to determine candidates for 1968, Larry Dutenhaver—one of

Concerned Citizens' strongest allies on the board who had delivered a stern rebuke to the conservative wing after the January 1967 elections—was not recommended for re-election.

In December, with another round of elections approaching, Concerned Citizens invited its supporters to a meeting to determine their path forward.

"During the last year," it explained, "LPCA has become less and less viable as an organization which speaks for the diverse community of people in Lincoln Park. It has become progressively more conservative." Responding to the removal of Reed and Dutenhaver from their posts, the letter went on: "At the time LPCA is concentrating on eliminating dissent...Spanish people, poor whites, and students are being pushed out of the community through higher rents, real estate speculation, rehabilitation and building of townhouses."

And yet, once again, Concerned Citizens decided to try to gain influence and power within LPCA. Concerned Citizens launched their own slate of candidates for office, with Rev. Reed at the top of the ticket for president. Their platform promised the governance reforms they had pushed a year earlier and more affordable housing.

But when January came, the results were even more lopsided than in 1967: 433 for the incumbent Roland Whitman to fifty-nine for Reed. Definitively rejected by LPCA's membership, anti-displacement activists in 1968 would move away from attempts to reform the Association, and start trying to defeat it.

Ironically, the failure of Reed's pro-low-income housing candidacy was followed by an LPCA campaign to double the amount of government-subsidized housing in Project One. The campaign, however, was less about blunting the effect of displacement on low-income residents than mitigating the problems the private market had created for middle-class families.

Under the original plan, two-thirds of the sites cleared by

the urban renewal program were to be redeveloped privately at market prices. Given the housing market in and around the Old Town Triangle, everyone understood that meant that two-thirds of the redevelopment sites would be priced for middle- and upper-income households.

But as time went on, the rehabbers realized that there was a problem with this plan: the market was not building the kinds of housing they wanted. The time had long passed when most renovations were done by couples looking to join a community of creative do-it-yourselfers, or even small-time professional developers. Left to their own devices, the new, larger developers essentially built two kinds of homes.

The first were a higher-end version of the small one-bedroom and studio apartments that LPCA had spent the last fifteen years trying to stamp out with the strict enforcement campaign. Built in high-rises along the lake and boxy five-story buildings inland, they filled primarily with "transient" young white collar workers who many rehabbers considered a nuisance.

The second were single-family townhouses that fit LPCA's model of the ideal home much more closely. But land costs in Old Town had risen to such an extent—from about $150 per front foot in the late 1950s to as much as $700 per front foot in 1968—that newly built townhomes were priced beyond even the means of the middle- and upper-middle-class professionals who made up the core of the Association's membership.

LPCA's solution was to add six new locations for subsidized housing targeted at "moderate" income families, making close to average Chicago wages. The original Project One plan called for six subsidized housing sites: three for moderate income households, and three for low-income public housing. The new proposal would double the total number of subsidized sites, but without increasing the options for the lowest-income households who were most rapidly being pushed from the neighborhood.

Rev. Reed and Concerned Citizens of Lincoln Park attacked LPCA's plan as too little, too late for the scale of displacement. "Six sites...are but a timid step towards providing adequate housing," Concerned Citizens wrote in a flyer. "Six sites are swell: Sixty are sufficient."

The plan also received pushback from conservative rehabbers who felt Lincoln Park was still on a tipping point between middle-class stability and urban slum, and that any kind of subsidized housing would put weight on the wrong end of the scale. "Private rehabilitation stopped the deterioration of housing in Lincoln Park," one resident objected at a hearing on the plan. "Excess subsidized housing...benefits one segment of the community to the detriment of the entire area."

Meanwhile, the Mid-North Association warned that "excess of moderate income housing would unbalance the diversity of the student body" at local grade schools, "and discourage middle income families from remaining."

But it was concern for schools that may have pushed most rehabbers to endorse the proposal. By 1968, enrollment at elementary schools in the Project One area was cratering. In 1966, 820 students had attended LaSalle Elementary; in 1968, only 540 registered. Nearby Lincoln Elementary had just two-thirds of its normal enrollment. With funding based in part on attendance, they were faced with the possibility of losing staff positions, including librarians and gym teachers.

The reasons were clear enough: Urban renewal had demolished the homes of hundreds of local families, and private renovators were continuing to deconvert multi-family apartment buildings into fewer, larger units, or single-family homes. Meanwhile, new market housing was not making much of a difference. The smaller apartments filled with young people without school-age children, and the families who bought the high-end townhomes were wealthy enough to pay for tuition at prestigious private schools.

The final compromise, reached in July after several months of public hearings and private negotiations, did double the number of sites for subsidized housing. In terms of units, subsidized housing increased from about forty percent to almost sixty percent of all the housing to be built on cleared Project One land. The proportion of family units was also increased.

On the other hand, these changes were offset somewhat by the fact that the total number of homes to be built was reduced by about a tenth. In other words, subsidized housing made up a larger share of a smaller pie. And while LPCA was eager to increase the number of family-sized homes in moderate-income developments, they kept the vast majority of low-income public housing restricted to the elderly. Before, Project One had called for just eighteen units of family-sized public housing; now, it called for sixty, in an area where thousands of qualifying households had been displaced. Even the total number of income-restricted homes, at about 600, represented a fraction of those displaced by public demolition, let alone private renovations.

Changes to Project One were not the only way that LPCA tried to steer Lincoln Park's housing market in their preferred directions. Though protests sometimes broke out over the high-rises that developers periodically proposed along a narrow lakeside strip, zoning laws banned such dense housing in the vast majority of Lincoln Park. As a result, rehabbers focused much more intently on the low-rise apartments that were being erected across much of the neighborhood.

In April, a working group formed to address one especially hated kind of development: the four plus one. These were apartment buildings with a partially below-ground level of parking under four floors of apartments, usually skewed towards studios and one-bedrooms and targeted to young white-collar renters. They generally left no setback on either side of their lots, and presented the street with a plain brick rectangle with minimal decoration.

Rehabbers objected to what they saw as the buildings' ugliness. But just as importantly, if not more so, four plus ones seemed to represent the return of a kind of housing that they had spent years trying to eliminate.

Reversing the pattern that had dominated in Old Town for two decades, four plus ones often replaced larger apartments and single-family homes with a much greater number of smaller units. This meant homes for renters, singles, and childless couples, rather than homeowning families.

"Glorified rooming houses and a potential slum situation," was the verdict from one of the organizers of the new group. Another, marching in the demonstration that kicked off the anti-four plus one campaign, held a sign that read: "4+1s = Tomorrow's Slums." LPCA's newsletter, in an article about the budding campaign to kill the four plus one, analogized them to another type of housing it christened the "slave quarter duplex."

The "slum" term referred partly to the rehabbers' fear that high-density buildings were necessarily undesirable. But it also referred to relatively lower-cost housing, and the kinds of people who might live in it. Though not nearly as cheap as the rapidly dwindling number of old unrenovated buildings, an apartment in a four plus one was substantially cheaper than a renovated Victorian or new townhome, the styles that rehabbers put at the top of the housing hierarchy. And unlike high-rises, which had to be built with steel or concrete, the cheaper materials used in four plus ones meant that they sometimes offered rents as much as forty percent below those in the towers a few blocks away.

For many rehabbers, the affordability was not a positive. One opponent, talking to the *Tribune*, worried that the managers of four plus ones might be "less selective about their tenants." Many were concerned that the greater density of "transient" renters, combined with the buildings' appearance, would damage their property values.

The new working group's goal was to eliminate them through new zoning provisions, requiring more parking spaces than could fit under the buildings, more expensive construction techniques, and setbacks on either side (though townhomes would be exempt from the setback provision). Within a few years, this drive would be successful.

CHAPTER 7
THE POOR PEOPLE'S COALITION

As the rehabbers' strategies evolved during 1968, the focus of anti-displacement activism was changing as well. To a great extent, two new leaders brought about these changes. Pat Devine had been hired as a full-time organizer for Concerned Citizens to give the group more focus. A young resident of Lincoln Park who had moved from suburban Aurora, Devine had only learned of the urban renewal program in 1966, after she became involved with a progressive church group where Rev. Reed also worked. Under her leadership, the anti-displacement group gained a new outspokenness and independence from the mainstream rehabbers.

Devine launched a monthly newsletter, the "Lincoln Park Press," to compete for eyes and minds with the one published by LPCA. While LPCA's paper carried "progress reports" about the number of buildings demolished or renovated, Lincoln Park Press carried a "Demolition Scorecard" on the front of each issue.

"Families…who had to leave Lincoln Park because of Urban Renewal: 939," the Scorecard read in the Press' second issue in January 1968. "Families…able to remain in Lincoln Park: 272." Just above was a story with the headline, "LPCA Refuses to Act on Community Issues."

Devine also began organizing residents to attend every Community Council meeting—particularly those who lived in areas that might be voted for demolition. And it was while she was preparing for one of these meetings that she met Cha Cha Jiménez.

Jiménez—whose given name was José—was still a teenager in 1968. His parents were migrant workers who had raised him on the Near North Side until they were displaced by urban renewal and landed in Lincoln Park. As an adolescent, he rose in the ranks of the Young Lords, a Puerto Rican gang that had been organized as protection against the area's older Italian and Appalachian street gangs. In 1964, he became its leader. But he also was in and out of jail on fighting and drug charges.

While serving a sixty-day drug sentence in the spring of 1968, Jiménez became captivated by political and philosophical writings, including those of a Trappist monk, Martin Luther King, and Malcolm X. By the time he left prison in August, he was thinking about how to reshape the Young Lords into something more than a street gang.

Lincoln Park in the summer of 1968 was a fertile ground for new radical organizations. The Democratic National Convention arrived in Chicago in August, and a storm of protesters from across the country descended on the city, many camping out in Lincoln Park. (LPCA, still self-consciously aligned with progressivism, passed a resolution asking the police to allow them to stay.) Soon after he returned, Jiménez attended a rally where Black Panther Party chairman Bobby Seale spoke about the BPP's approach to radical organizing within black communities. Jiménez decided to refound the Young Lords on the model of the Black Panthers' ideology and organization.

Jiménez himself admitted that the transformation wasn't easy. Most of his followers were teenagers, many not even out of high school, and his new revolutionary philosophy did not always find easy converts. But many had experienced the displacement of urban renewal firsthand—including Jiménez, whose family moved nine times—as well as discrimination as Puerto Ricans. By September—officially September 23, the hundredth anniversary of the "Grito de Lares," Puerto Rico's first revolt against Spanish rule—Jiménez refounded the Young Lords as the Young Lords Organization, a political group that would fight for radical social and political change in Lincoln Park and beyond.

Soon after, Jiménez became acquainted with Concerned Citizens. According to Devine, she and a number of other residents were on a sidewalk, working on posters for an upcoming protest of a Community Council meeting. Jiménez asked about the posters; Devine invited him to come to the meeting. He was shocked at who was in the room to make decisions about whose homes would stay and whose would be torn down.

"I didn't see a black face, nor a Puerto Rican face, not even a poor white's face in the whole meeting," Jiménez wrote in YLO's newsletter afterwards. "I asked why there was no one from the community, and they said it was hard to get anyone to come... I told Dick Vission [another Concerned Citizens organizer] and Pat Devine to find out when the next meeting was and I would get some people to come."

The year 1969 would not be like any previous year in Lincoln Park's conservation history, mostly because the Young Lords Organization was not like any anti-urban renewal group the neighborhood had seen before. The first wave of sustained, organized opposition to urban renewal, from about 1964 to 1965, centered around groups like the Larrabee Street Improvement Association, which fought the demolition called for by Project One with protests and letter-writing campaigns. The second wave, lasting into 1968, centered on the growing dissent within LPCA itself about the direction conservation was taking in Lincoln Park. Though their rhetoric could be harsh, these dissenters, led by people like Rev. James Reed, generally either worked through LPCA's formal internal channels or took up conventional outside pressure campaigns like pickets and leaflets.

The rise of YLO—often with the support of Pat Devine's Concerned Citizens group—marked the beginning of a third phase. Once again, organized opposition to urban renewal in Lincoln Park moved outside of LPCA. But YLO and Concerned Citizens also adopted a radical revolutionary ideology and confrontational, disruptive tactics that deeply unsettled Lincoln Park rehabbers and downtown urban renewal officials—and they eventually sought to drive the redevelopment of the community under their own control.

In response, some Lincoln Park conservatives adopted increasingly extreme tactics of their own to try to shut them down. Those, in turn, led to growing condemnations from the more liberal rehabbers. The Lincoln Park Conservation Association had entered the 1960s triumphantly, seemingly on the cusp of turning its bold plan for the neighborhood into reality. But as the decade closed, that idealism had been worn down under its own contradictions and finally flattened by the voices of those LPCA aimed to evict.

Cha Cha Jiménez only needed to attend one conservation meeting to make everyone aware that he was leading a different kind of resistance. In January, Jiménez brought a few dozen young YLO members, most of whom were only just learning the details of Lincoln Park's renewal plans, to the Department of Urban Renewal office on Larrabee Street. Before the meeting began, they noticed a model of the neighborhood, highlighting areas slated for redevelopment in Phase Two. When many of them went to look for their blocks, they found them blank, their homes already gone from the display.

That was enough. Someone flipped the table the model sat on; others took chairs and ran them through the Department of Urban Renewal's front windows. The police were called, but the Young Lords fled before anyone was arrested.

"It woke folks up," Pat Devine said later. "We had been demonstrating very nicely…because the churches were behind the opposition movement. Now we had these young people, and their whole style of operating was much different."

The Department of Urban Renewal, and many rehabbers, had a somewhat different reaction. Lewis Hill, the Department's longtime commissioner, used a speech a few weeks later at DePaul University to make his position clear.

"Joint public and private efforts have been able to help restore the Lincoln Park area to its rightful place as one of the city's most popular residential communities," he declared. But that progress was threatened by "the basically anti-social violent orientation of certain groups."

"We have opposed their terror tactics in the past," Hill said. "And we will continue to do so in the future, even though greed, or willfulness, is masked as concern for 'the people.'"

Despite the harsh words, LPCA and the Community Council did make some conciliatory moves during the first few months of 1969. In January, Roland Whitman was replaced as LPCA president by Stephen Shamberg. A 29-year-old lawyer who had worked for a legal clinic serving residents of the Cabrini-Green public housing complex, Shamberg was more sympathetic to critics of the urban renewal process and LPCA's legitimacy than his predecessor.

Addressing the Association's annual meeting in January, he promised that LPCA would work more proactively with residents to shape renewal and developments plans. He quickly followed through by increasing the number of meetings open to all LPCA members from one to four a year, a longtime demand of Concerned Citizens and other critics. In February, when the Community Council's only Latino member, Felix Silva, resigned to protest the Council's lack of diversity, the remaining Council members—all of whom were also members of LPCA—voted unanimously to ask Mayor Daley to appoint more Latino, black, and poor white members.

Still, LPCA continued to frequently see things through a distinctly middle-class lens. Often, Executive Director Patrick Feely was the one to express this perspective. Despite his youth and appearance—the *Tribune* described his clothes as "a few hues and inches beyond Ivy League"—Feely was more aligned with the conservative wing of the Association. Early in the year, for example, when the LPCA board approved several moderate-income family rowhomes on Larrabee, Feely's comments to the *Tribune* were largely critical. His criticism focused not on the fact that the project had provided only six homes, but that the homes were, in his view, substandard.

"The living rooms are so small, it would be impossible for a family of six even to watch television all at one time," he said. Moreover, there wasn't enough storage room. Where, he asked, would the the displaced families who bought these homes put their lawnmowers?

Meanwhile, the tentative steps made by Shamberg and the Community Council did little to mollify their increasingly radical opposition. Concerned Citizens released a new, broader list of demands. They included a majority share of poor people, blacks, and Latinos on the Community Council; an end to evictions and rent increases; and rent-restricted subsidized housing on all land that had already been cleared. In March, Pat Devine rechristened Concerned Citizens of Lincoln Park as the Concerned Citizens Survival Front, an organization that would stop treating the rehabbers' institutions as targets of reform, but as enemies to be ignored, dominated, or removed.

"People are getting angry at being overlooked," she wrote to Lyle Mayer, the Community Council's chairman, in April after learning he had organized a planning workshop without Concerned Citizens. Listing her own group along with other organizations of single mothers, Appalachians, churches, and YLO, she added: "The following groups will be present at the workshop…. You no longer have anything to say about who can and who can't participate in the workshop…. It's the decision of the people."

Over the course of the year, the Young Lords would become increasingly targeted by law enforcement and public officials as dangerous radicals. But they also faced the kind of discrimination and violence that young people of color routinely confronted in Chicago. On the evening of May 3, the Young Lords threw a birthday party at a home in the South Side neighborhood of Bridgeport. James Lamb, an off-duty police officer, came out of his house across the street to complain about the noise. He began to fight with a YLO member named Manuel Ramos, then took out a gun and began shooting. Ramos was killed on the spot; another person was shot but survived. Four Young Lords were arrested for aggravated battery, but the state's attorney declared that Lamb's use of force was justified, and he was never charged.

The Young Lords responded to Ramos' killing with a new organizing effort. After the wake, YLO led a 75-car caravan from Lincoln Park to Bridgeport, and held a press conference in front of Mayor Daley's bungalow there. A few days later, at the funeral, a packed Lincoln Park church listened to speeches by members of the Young Lords, along with representative of the Black Panthers and the Young Patriots, a radical organization of southern whites.

The next week, YLO made by far its biggest move to date. Around midnight on Wednesday, May 14, about a dozen

Young Lords and Concerned Citizens organizers broke into the administration building at McCormick Theological Seminary, a liberal religious institution a few blocks north of the Project One boundaries, near DePaul University. They barricaded themselves inside, hung a banner naming the building after Manuel Ramos, and demanded support for their anti-displacement campaign in exchange for leaving peacefully.

McCormick was a curious choice; up to that point, it had neither taken advantage of any lands cleared by urban renewal, nor made any requests to do so. But at least one observer thought it was a savvy target. A columnist for the *Lerner Booster*, one of a network of neighborhood papers, pointed out that LPCA leaders reported to a large membership that was resistant or hostile to outside criticism. McCormick, on the other hand, was made up of administrators, faculty, and students who all believed that a reputation for progressive leadership was key to the success of the institution.

After five days of occupation, the gamble paid off. Under pressure from many of the seminary's students, who had publicly sided with the Young Lords, McCormick announced it would meet many of the occupiers' demands. It would pass a resolution urging the investigation of James Lamb for the murder of Manuel Ramos; formally join the progressive church group in which the Rev. James Reed was active; and, perhaps most consequentially, furnish some $280,000 to capitalize an affordable housing development effort led by YLO and other local activist groups.

YLO declared victory and released the building. But the summer of high-stakes standoffs between YLO, Concerned Citizens, and their allies on one side; and LPCA, the Community Council, and the Department of Urban Renewal on the other were just beginning.

Just days later, at the Community Council's May meeting, YLO and Concerned Citizens would score another major win. In some ways, it would mark the high point of their fight against renewal.

Since January's protest over the Council's lack of diversity, seven new members had been appointed to its fifteen seats, including two black members and an additional Latino member. But neither Concerned Citizens nor YLO were satisfied with that progress.

As the meeting began, Young Lords and Young Patriots flanked one wall of the auditorium at Waller High School. Before the chair, Lyle Mayer, could officially call it into session, they began to chant "Resign!" so loudly he could not be heard. Stopping to allow one protester to speak, they announced to the crowd: "This meeting cannot continue until poor people are represented on the council!"

Eventually, Mayer was able to start the meeting. But once he had, one of the newly appointed members, Richard Brown, took over. Brown, a leader with a community organization in Lincoln Park's southwest corner called the Neighborhood Commons Corporation, was one of the newly appointed black members to the Conservation Community Council. Now, he introduced a rapid series of motions calling for the resignation of each "unrepresentative" Council member. His fellow members duly voted down each resolution.

But the disruption seemed to rattle the Council. Before the meeting closed, it made a few crucial concessions to the anti-displacement protesters.

First, Mayer could return to regular order only by handing the floor to a tavern owner whose Larrabee Street building—one of the last standing on an already-cleared block—had been slated for demolition and redevelopment. After a long anti-urban renewal speech, the Community Council voted to ask the city to rescind the sale of his property to a developer, ignoring the objections of a Department of Urban Renewal official who claimed they had no power to make such a request.

The Community Council then took up a critical resolution: a moratorium on demolition in Phase Two until the people already displaced by renewal had been rehoused. Formally introduced by Lincoln Park's Independent Political Organization, a recently formed group that included some of the liberal wing of LPCA, such a moratorium had long been central to the demands of the more radical groups like YLO and Concerned Citizens.

After some discussion, Community Coucil passed the resolution. It was an incredible victory: Direct displacement by urban renewal had seemingly been stopped in its tracks.

———————————

In addition to high-profile political demonstrations, Cha Cha Jiménez wanted the Young Lords to follow the Black Panthers' example in providing direct community services to Puerto Ricans and others living in Lincoln Park. YLO's major priorities included a free daycare center, free breakfast program, support for evicted tenants, and a health clinic. But each of these would require more room than YLO had at the storefront they operated out of, and so Jiménez went looking for space.

The most obvious choice seemed to be the Armitage Avenue Methodist Church, which sat just a block from the heart of the Lincoln Park Puerto Rican community at Armitage and Halsted. Its pastor, Bruce Johnson, had been assigned to Armitage Avenue the previous summer after a few years in Humboldt Park, a West Side neighborhood where many Puerto Ricans had settled in the early 1960s. Clean-cut and not yet thirty, Johnson embraced a progressive mission there, opening a community center near Armitage and Kedzie—three miles west of Halsted—with the help of James Reed.

Jiménez had approached Johnson about using the Armitage Avenue church's basement for Young Lords Organization services earlier in the year. Johnson had demurred, citing strong opposition from some members of his congregation, particularly Cuban immigrants, who considered YLO a communist group. In June, however, a group of Young Lords decided to simply move into the basement without Jiménez's knowledge, and declared it open for community service operations. When the police arrived, called by alarmed parishioners, Johnson turned them away, effectively endorsing the occupation and giving the Young Lords a permanent home base in the neighborhood.

Those not inclined to sympathize with the Young Lords or their allies, however, watched Armitage Avenue Methodist with growing alarm.

These concerns had grown after the May Community Council meeting.

"That meeting was a turning point, for me, in terms of defining legitimate dissent," LPCA president Stephen Shamberg told the *Tribune*. In a letter to LPCA members, Shamberg wrote that the disruptions of YLO, Concerned Citizens, and other activists were an "attack on the democratic process led by persons one writer aptly characterized as 'pseudo-revolutionary middle-class totalitarians,'" he wrote.

Rev. Johnson's acceptance of these "totalitarians" in a religious institution like the Armitage Avenue Methodist Church provoked a fierce backlash. Within weeks of the McCormick Seminary occupation, a campaign had begun to cut off the Armitage Avenue church from the larger Methodist organization, or find a new pastor who would cut off the YLO. The Mid-North Association wrote to the Bishop of the North Illinois Conference of the Methodist Church, expressing alarm and warning that Rev. Johnson was "fester[ing] revolutionaries."

One of Lincoln Park's aldermen, George McCutcheon, joined these protests. He pointed not just to Rev. Johnson's church, but to Rev. Reed, who, he warned the Bishop, was "increasingly involved with violent dissidence." But for months, neither the alderman nor the Mid-North Association received any response—a silence that only increased their frustration.

Meanwhile, there were indications that the Community Council might be reneging on its demolition moratorium at its next meeting in July. Despite voting in May to wait for displaced people to be rehoused, the Council announced that it would take up the question of a new round of clearance and redevelopment. The streets targeted for demolition included some of the cheapest market-rate housing remaining in Lincoln Park, and also the most heavily populated by black residents. In some places near North Avenue, the housing would be replaced with parks and industrial zones as a kind of buffer between Lincoln Park and the Cabrini-Green area to the south.

Under one version of the plan, demolition would be delayed to rehouse those who would be displaced in new low-income homes planned for Larrabee Street. But that did little to mollify Concerned Citizens, YLO, and their allies, who were now operating under an umbrella called the "Poor People's Coalition."

Yet another flash point on the agenda concerned an empty lot at Armitage and Halsted that had been cleared under Project One. In the very different political environment of 1965, it had been designated for private recreational space, and the Department of Urban Renewal had solicited bids for a tennis club. But when details of the bids—including annual membership costing $1,500, or nearly a year's rent for a low-income family—were released in the summer of 1969, opposition exploded. Community Council members announced that they would ask the Department to withdraw the bid at the July meeting, but it would still need to be formally discussed.

That discussion did not take place. When the doors to the Waller High School auditorium opened, more than 500 people packed into the meeting. Almost immediately, a number of Young Lords jumped onto the stage to take it over; in the audience, YLO supporters and residents who wanted the meeting to continue threw punches and chairs. Meanwhile, protesters and members of the Council fought on the stage for the microphone, with chairman Lyle Mayer knocked to the ground by fellow Council member Richard Brown. The Council was dismissed before it could vote on either the demolitions or the tennis site.

If the May Community Council meeting had been a "turning point," in Shamberg's words, July was a rallying cry for those who opposed YLO, Concerned Citizens, and the rest of the Poor People's Coalition.

"Until we actually saw the militant, fascist manner in which the so-called 'poor people' conducted themselves, it was our sincere desire to aid these people," one block club from Burling Street wrote to Lyle Mayer in the days after the meeting. "[But] the general attitude of the homeowners as they left the meeting was, '…and that's what we're supposed to let live in our homes???'… We cannot…give them our neighborhood."

A common theme was incredulity that the middle-class residents of Lincoln Park had been singled out as villains. "None of us are 'rich people,'" the Burling block club wrote to Mayer. "We have worked diligently in maintaining our block…. We worked for the money for the down payments and the monthly mortgage payments." In fact, it was precisely because they were not "rich" that they could not afford to allow the presence of "poor people" to ruin their fragile economic standing. "We do not wish to run the poor people out of the area," they explained, "but neither can we afford to allow the investment that we have in our property…for which we worked to attain, be 'washed down the drain.'"

Lewis Hill, the head of the Department of Urban Renewal, also objected that he was simply doing what conservation demanded. If the DUR was involved in "tearing down housing that cannot be restored," he said in a speech to LPCA, "and this housing happens to be tenanted by the poor—with black or Spanish speaking—it does not mean that we are initiating a racist 'pogrom' or deliberately shifting whole social classes." If such a shift was taking place, he suggested, it was not meant to discriminate against the poor or people of color, but rather to sacrifice them to a higher cause.

Shamberg, too, joined this litany. "LPCA has been pictured by some as a principal oppressor of the poor in Lincoln Park," he wrote in an exasperated letter to its membership. The protesters claimed that "we are, individually, symbols of life's oppression." In fact, he insisted, the anti-renewal activists should have been grateful: "IF it had not been for LPCA...most probably Lincoln Park would have been bulldozed from end to end. We have helped create a...viable community where the individual can be heard.... If this were another part of Chicago, you would not be heard."

Still, Shamberg expressed deep misgivings about stoking the fires of resentment on both sides. "I fear that the events of the last few months are leading to a complete, probably irremediable, polarization," he wrote to LPCA members in early August. And polarization, he went on, might mean that the gears of urban renewal would stop—and no more urban renewal would mean "no new low income housing would be constructed. Private rehabilitation will occur, and rents will...be raised.... Any increase in rent drives a poor family out.... Our government must not be allowed to avoid providing low income housing because of the intense bitterness...in our community."

Shamberg's conclusion, however, seemed less a call for reconciliation than a cursing of all sides:

"To the professed 'liberals' in our community who ask that we forgive and forget...: Where have you been for the past seven months and how many doors have you broken down trying to get low income housing constructed in Lincoln Park? ...To those calling themselves 'moderates' and expressing 'concern' for the problems of the poor while deploring the tactics of the totalitarians: Isn't the unfettered free enterprise system…driving poor families from miserable housing to worse? What happened to the commitment to provide housing for those who have been displaced from our community?"

There were few indications, however, that either side was interested in anything but a harder fight. The Mid-North Association sent out letters asking for witnesses to come forward so that members of the Poor People's Coalition could be charged for assault and other crimes. Alderman McCutcheon and the Mid-North Association sent new letters to the Methodist Conference asking that something be done to stop the activities at Rev. Reed and Rev. Johnson's churches. Privately, Johnson was receiving hate mail, including death threats.

In August, a new showdown emerged. The Young Lords wanted to throw a block party at the Armitage Avenue Methodist Church, which they now called the People's Church. Anti-YLO residents collected petitions with over 300 signatures against the event, and Alderman McCutcheon denied the permit. When Jiménez went ahead with the festival without the permits, the police arrived, and another fight broke out as they tried to shut it down. In the end, the police arrested five Young Lords and several people on both sides were hospitalized.

———————

YLO had staked a claim to attention and power in large part thanks to its willingness to physically disrupt urban renewal proceedings. But by September, urban renewal officials were determined to reassert their own powers of physical intimidation. When the next scheduled Community Council meeting opened its doors, attendees were greeted by 100 uniformed police officers.

If Council members had been pushed towards anti-renewal votes by protesters in May, the show of police force in September seemed to embolden the Council's "moderate" majority. Reversing the landmark moratorium on new demolition passed just four months prior, the Community Council voted to allow purchase and clearance of properties if volunteered by their owners. Non-owners—including the renters who made up the vast majority of residents in the affected area—would not have a say, though they would be given priority in new housing constructed in Lincoln Park. Despite heckling from the audience, the meeting continued through its regular business from there, and adjourned without incident.

The tense order of the Council meeting, however, was followed by escalating acts of violence. On the morning of September 14, three days after the reversal of the demolition moratorium, Alderman McCutcheon's Lincoln Park offices were firebombed. So were those of Alderman William Singer, who also represented parts of Lincoln Park but who had been much more sympathetic to anti-urban renewal activists in his public remarks.

The Young Lords denied any involvement in the bombings, but McCutcheon blamed them. Three days later, he introduced an ordinance to the City Council calling for a greater police crackdown on the Young Lords' territory and a committee to investigate not just YLO, but the Methodist church's support for them.

That was enough to provoke a response from the Methodist hierarchy. It was not, however, the one McCutcheon and his allies were hoping for. "The church is seeking to perform a ministry of reconciliation for a desperately needy area," the Superintendent of the Chicago Northern District wrote, expressing his support for the Armitage Avenue church. "It is our conviction that this ministry to the Young Lord's Youth Organization…is being engaged in creatively and democratically." The same day, as if to drive the point home, Rev. Bruce Johnson held a press conference to defend YLO, and accused McCutcheon of "intemperance and prejudice" in his battle against them.

Exactly a week after the press conference, on the morning of September 29, a mailman found Bruce Johnson's four-year-old son on the front steps, crying, his feet bloody. He stepped inside the house to a horrific scene. Rev. Johnson lay in an easy chair in the living room, stabbed to death. The table next to him held two cups of coffee, as if he had been chatting with someone. In the bedroom, police found his wife's body, also stabbed to death, and a bloody butcher's knife.

Given the hate mail and death threats he had received, many of those who had fought side by side with Rev. Johnson assumed that he had been martyred by opponents of the radical anti-urban renewal activists. "These murders," a press release from the Young Lords Organization pronounced, "show to what vicious lengths the ruling class will go to prevent the growth of our just struggle." At his funeral, a few days later, more than two thousand people turned out. Many gathered at the corner of Halsted and Armitage— where, in place of the private tennis club, a group of Young Lords had constructed a makeshift "People's Park"—and marched to the service as a New Orleans funeral procession. Luis Cuza, who just a few years earlier had been one of the LPCA staffers instrumental in founding the more moderate Spanish American Federation, now expressed the sense of loss as a member of YLO: "He's one of the only North American whites who ever helped us out materially."

Despite the conviction of his allies that the killings were political, police insisted that they had no leads, clues, or suspects in the days afterwards, and no one was ever arrested. Johnson's enemies generally expressed regret, though at least some were willing to talk about how much they had hated him while he was alive. "We just feel he was detrimental the neighborhood," one person told the *Sun-Times* a day after the murders. "People who live around here were close to being enraged."

Then, very early on the morning of December 4, someone threw a firebomb into the basement of the Armitage Avenue Methodist Church, where YLO held its daycare and other events. Two passersby saw the smoke and were able to put out the fire before it caused major damage.

At the same time, several miles away, police were preparing a predawn raid on the West Side apartment of Fred Hampton, who had worked with YLO as chairman of the Illinois Black Panther Party. According to the police, Hampton and a Black Panther guard began to shoot at the officers, who shot back and killed them both. But a federal investigation would show that just one round had been fired from the Panthers' gun, to as many as 99 from the police, and that a number of other claims by the police at the raid did not hold up to scrutiny. Photos of his bloody mattress showed that Hampton had probably been fatally shot before he got out of bed.

Hampton was the third prominent member or ally of the Young Lords Organization to be killed in 1969. Like Manuel Ramos and Bruce Johnson, his death both deeply shook YLO members and allies and created a rallying cry that galvanized further action.

In fact, YLO and the rest of the Poor People's Coalition were on the verge of their most ambitious project yet. Rather than demanding that urban renewal officials manage the neighborhood differently, they would spend the next several months fighting to take direct control of a piece of Lincoln Park's redevelopment.

The Monday after the Hampton raid, PPC formally submitted a bid to build on a cleared urban renewal parcel. Using money they had received from the May occupation of McCormick Theological Seminary, the PPC had formed a development corporation and hired an architect to design a complex with seventy apartments. Forty percent, the maximum allowed by federal regulations, would be restricted to low-income tenants.

The bid was audacious for a number of reasons. Not least, certainly, was that in order to be considered by City Hall, it first had to receive the recommendation of the Lincoln Park Conservation Community Council—just months after members of the Poor People's Coalition had violently shut down Community Council meetings.

Yet early indications were that the Council was leaning towards their bid. Lyle Mayer, who had chaired the Council for more than seven years, resigned in November, citing exhaustion after the contentious year. Replacing him was Stephen Shamberg, who in turn resigned his position as president of LPCA. Despite calling the activists "totalitarians" earlier in the year, Shamberg believed that PPC's proposal offered a way to bring the community back together by giving the working class residents most affected by urban renewal direct power to rebuild Lincoln Park according to their own vision. In January, he and the rest of the Council would have the opportunity to vote to grant them that power.

One reason that the PPC found sympathizers among liberal rehabbers was the way in which the events of 1969 had powerfully damaged the reputation of LPCA, both within and outside the organization. Towards the end of the year, a team of researchers from DePaul interviewed Lincoln Parkers about the role of the Association, and found that it had lost its legitimacy as a community voice not just for working class tenants or radical activists, but for some of its oldest champions.

Marshall Scott, a former president of LPCA, told a team of researchers from DePaul that the real troubles had started a few years earlier, when James Reed's campaign for reform within the Association was quashed. "[It] got caught at the time when land clearance came and you began to get people who were being pushed out rising up. The more LPCA was confronted with an issue, the more [then-president Roland Whitman] would sit on it. It just about collapsed."

For others, more recent events gave a cynical tint to LPCA's long-professed ideals. A camera store owner in Old Town who had been a board member dismissed the Association's commitment to "diversity." "Its meaning depends on who is saying it," he explained. "Diversity for upper class people means cobblestone streets and a tennis club on Armitage and Halsted."

But perhaps the most devastating criticism came from Malcolm Shanower. Shanower was as close as LPCA had to an elder statesman. He had been in the room where, all the way back in 1954, LPCA had been born; he had served as its executive director in the late 1950s. But by 1969 he had no use for it.

"Before, the board of directors had men on it who were dedicated," he told the researchers. "LPCA has now come to pretty bleak days in terms of moving social change for the community. It just can't understand or hear or deal with any of the criticism that might have made it thrive."

There were defenders of LPCA and the rehabbers' neighborhood organizations as well. But they could sound even more cynical than the detractors. "LPCA wants an integrated community only to a degree," said Donald Howe, the president of the Park West Association, part of LPCA north of Old Town. "And there already is a black area on the edge of Lincoln Park." (Howe was referring to the area north of Cabrini Green, a significant part of which Phase Two called to be demolished.)

As for economic integration, Howe concluded: "There are other areas of the city where [the] poor can live."

In this context, the Poor People's Coalition bid to take control of the redevelopment of Lincoln Park was a kind of showdown between radical anti-renewal activists and their liberal sympathizers, and the more conservative members of the community who sought to defeat them once and for all.

The Poor People's Coalition faced one other serious bidder for their redevelopment site, a more traditional developer called Hartford Construction. In many ways, Hartford's proposal was similar to PPC's: a mix of market-rate and rent-restricted apartments in a low-rise building. It differed in the income mix and architectural design.

The Coalition intended to set aside as high a proportion of low-income units as possible—up to forty percent under HUD regulations—at rents as low as possible. If HUD would negotiate with them after they won the bid, they said, they would try to get a 100 percent low-income building. Hartford, on the other hand, began with twenty percent, before increasing to forty percent when it became clear that Community Council would look favorably on a greater amount of affordable housing. Anything beyond that, the company insisted, would be counterproductive.

Architecturally, the Hartford proposal followed the standard modern, boxy designs of other new developments in Lincoln Park. But the Poor People's Coalition architect, Howard Alan, abandoned this template for a striking design with apartments lining a series of cascading terraces. Rather than using fences to divide the terraces into private porches, the proposal kept them open, creating a kind of quasi-public space that several households would share. The idea was to design for a communal style of living that PPC believed was more natural for the working class families they wanted to serve, rather than more middle-class expectations of privacy.

The rehabbers divided on both of these distinctions. While some believed Lincoln Park needed as much low-income housing as possible, others argued that too much risked pushing the neighborhood back into a "slum." Skeptics pointed out that the site lay just blocks from the poor neighborhood around Cabrini-Green on the other side of North Avenue. An all-low-income development in Lincoln Park would just bring a "ghetto mentality" across North, LPCA's Executive Director Pat Feely said.

The design, too, rubbed some the wrong way. Though it was considered innovative by many—Walter Netsch, an Old Town resident and architect who had designed the campus of the University of Illinois at Chicago, said the terraces "reflected the independent goals of middle income people and the interdependent goals of the poor"—others believed the shared terraces were ugly and would hurt property values.

But really, the most controversial part of the Poor People's Coalition bid was the Coalition itself. For many white, middle class Lincoln Parkers, the collection of activists behind the project needed to be driven out of the neighborhood, not rewarded with greater control over a piece of it. They were, in the circumspect words of the Old Town Triangle Association, "interests unsympathetic to community preservation."

Both sides understood that the stakes of the Poor People's Coalition bid were about more than just the fate of a single housing development. They were also about whether the informal power structure that had controlled urban renewal in Lincoln Park from the start would continue to do so.

Formally, the chain of command began with the Lincoln Park Conservation Community Council, which relayed the official preference of the neighborhood to the Department of Urban Renewal. The Department, then, would take the local recommendation into account with other information and make up its own mind.

In practice, the Department of Urban Renewal almost never made a recommendation that contradicted the Community Council. And the Community Council almost never made a recommendation that contradicted LPCA, which had no formal role in the process at all. LPCA brought urban renewal to Lincoln Park in 1956, and through January of 1970 it had remained firmly in the driver's seat. But now its power seemed uncertain.

On the question of the proposed development, LPCA and its affiliated neighborhood groups, including the Old Town Triangle Association, stood firmly against the Poor People's Coalition. The

Coalition, LPCA charged, was not "a legitimate representative of the poor," but "a group of radicals." Their housing bid was an attempt "to enhance their power at the expense of community harmony and grassroots participation."

LPCA brought this position—and 1,000 petition signatures against the Poor People's Coalition, collected by former Community Council chair Lyle Mayer—to the Council meeting in January. But they did not receive their usual deference.

As recently as March of the year before, LPCA had controlled all but one seat on the Council. But the replacement of several members that spring to increase the Council's diversity, and the replacement of Council chair Lyle Mayer with Stephen Shamberg in December, had broken LPCA's hold. Led by Shamberg, the Council voted 11-2 in favor of the Poor People's Coalition.

LPCA, shocked at being overruled by the Council, challenged its legitimacy. Lyle Mayer said the vote was "an attempt to buy peace instead of an evaluation on [the] merits." Pointing to their stacks of petitions and the longstanding authority of LPCA as a representative of Lincoln Parkers, the rehabbers accused the Community Council of turning its back on the neighborhood.

But if the Council had broken the long-established power of LPCA, all was not lost for the rehabbers—because the city's Department of Urban Renewal was about to break the long-established authority of the Council.

The Department's final decision would be made by its board, which was scheduled to vote in February. Just weeks before the vote, however, the Department's staff went public with their recommendation: reject the Community Council's choice and approve the Hartford bid.

The reasons were supposedly apolitical, with Department staff suggesting that Hartford was the more financially stable bidder. But supporters of the Poor People's Coalition were outraged. At a press conference, seven of the Council members who voted for the

Coalition's bid—including LPCA cofounder Malcolm Shanower and former LPCA president Marvin Rosner, standing side by side with Richard Brown, who was under indictment for assaulting Lyle Mayer at the June Community Council meeting—threatened to quit in protest if the DUR reversed their decision. "If the DUR rejects our recommendations," Rosner told the press, "we cease to function as representatives of Lincoln Park and will have no alternative but to resign."

Their cause attracted citywide attention. In an editorial the day of the Department of Urban Renewal's board vote, the *Chicago Sun-Times* took the side of the Community Council and the Poor People's Coalition. "The right and ability of a neighborhood community to work on its own problems and guide its own destiny is at stake," the paper wrote under the headline "Housing By and For the Poor." "The decision seems to hinge on architectural considerations…. The Poor People's architectural concept is more responsive to the needs of the poor."

But when 300 agitated spectators crowded into the City Hall chambers on February 11, the Department's board voted unanimously in favor of Hartford Construction. PPC's supporters in the audience erupted. As the decision was announced, one man charged the board, but was restrained; fifteen more people were arrested, including one for throwing a three-foot-long metal "no smoking" sign at the dais.

The Poor People's Coalition and their supporters denounced the decision, and promised to ask the City Council to reverse it. The Department's vote "ran roughshod over the wishes of the people of the Lincoln Park area," the *Sun-Times* wrote. Marvin Rosner, speaking for the seven Community Council members who had threatened to resign, accused the Hartford plan of "using federal funds" to further the "economic segregation" of Lincoln Park. Even one Lincoln Park alderman, William Singer, took the Coalition's side. "Here were people who were told, 'Stop disrupting and try to be constructive. Work through the system.' So they chose that path.... And then in ten seconds it was all written off."

Ultimately, the City Council wrote them off too. In June, its housing committee voted to endorse the Department of Urban Renewal's recommendation in favor of Hartford. And while many backers of the Poor People's Coalition stuck by their side, other crucial allies did not. Stephen Shamberg, who had "betrayed" LPCA just a month after resigning its presidency to endorse the Poor People's Coalition bid back in January, announced at the City Council vote that he had changed his mind. The arrests at the February Department of Urban Renewal meeting, he said, proved that the Coalition was unfit to lead such a project.

And according to the *Tribune*, defeating the Poor People's Coalition bid had become a priority for city officials for larger reasons. There was "a fear by the city administration that an award to the Poor People's Coalition, with its history of disruptive tactics, would possibly set a precedent...for forcing demands upon the city." If the Coalition were successful, people elsewhere in Chicago might think they, too, could win concessions by not playing by the rules.

———————————

The fight over the future of Lincoln Park did not end with the defeat of the Poor People's Coalition housing bid. But in many ways, it marked the end of an era, the last skirmish in a battle that pitted the inheritors of the rehabbers' dreams of the 1940s and 1950s against the radicals and residents threatened with displacement who organized for their own vision of the neighborhood.

For Concerned Citizens and the Young Lords Organization, the loss suggested that they could neither beat the system from the outside, nor coopt it from the inside. Years' worth of organizing and disrupted meetings had earned some concessions, but hadn't stopped the renewal program or brought a meaningfully greater amount of affordable housing. A serious proposal to work within the renewal process to take responsibility for the neighborhood's redevelopment had shown that the people in power distrusted and feared them too much to let them in.

Pat Devine, who had been instrumental in leading Concerned Citizens for years, left Chicago entirely for California in the summer of 1970. Cha Cha Jiménez, founder of the Young Lords Organization, left Chicago as well in December, fleeing charges that he had stolen from a lumber yard. He returned to the city, and to activism, in 1972, even launching a campaign for alderman the next year. But it was in a ward in Lakeview, not Lincoln Park, fully two miles north of the old neighborhood around Armitage and Halsted. YLO continued work in Lincoln Park, but its focus moved from housing to healthcare, as it worked to set up a free health clinic.

For the Lincoln Park Conservation Association, the final defeat of the Poor People's Coalition bid was a victory that could only partially make up for the damage the fight had inflicted. LPCA would continue to exist, but as a different, and smaller, kind of organization. It had been disowned by some of its most prominent former leaders and denounced in the press as heartless and out of touch. It had been condemned by the editorial board of a major daily newspaper. And it had been humiliated by the Community Council, formally rejected as a legitimate voice of the neighborhood it claimed to represent, only to be lifted to victory by the downtown bureaucrats it had once claimed to stand apart from.

For many liberal Lincoln Parkers, the Association's reputation was dealt a new blow in December, when newspapers reported that its young Executive Director, Pat Feely, had accused dozens of Lincoln Park activists, businesses, and churches of being national security threats in testimony to the United States Senate Internal Security Subcommittee. Fights at Waller High School and the City

Council chambers were one thing; making lists of your neighbors for a Senate panel meant to expose communist infiltration was quite another. A flurry of members protested, threatening to quit in disgust, but the Association's board president stuck with Feely. These scandals and the winding down of federal support for urban renewal shrank LPCA's presence in the neighborhood to a single paid administrator by 1974, compared to a peak of ten paid staff in the 1960s.

And for both sides, there was the simple fact that the neighborhood had continued to change around them, even as they fought over its direction. The 1970 Census confirmed that the changes that had begun in earnest in the 1950s had profoundly accelerated in the 1960s. Rehabbing activity, the deconversion of small apartments, and smaller households had cut Lincoln Park's population from 102,000 in 1950 to 88,000 in 1960; by 1970, it had plunged to 68,000. Lincoln Park, in other words, was home to a third fewer people than it had been at the start of the conservation movement. Only a small part of that decline could be explained by urban renewal demolition, which had torn down about 2,000 housing units; the vast majority was private rehabilitation.

On the eastern half of the neighborhood, the rehabbers' strongholds had expanded and grown dramatically wealthier. Lincoln Park's lakefront areas were now among the richest tenth of the greater Chicago region, beating out even many newer suburbs. Away from the lake and north of Armitage Avenue, around DePaul University, incomes were also rising fast. In the Old Town Triangle, close to half of adults now were college graduates—compared to just about eight percent citywide. The Triangle remained ninety-five percent white, even as black and Latino Chicagoans now made up more than forty percent of city residents.

But south of Armitage and east of Larrabee—that is, on the other side of the divisions created by conservation demolition—trends were moving in the opposite direction. That end of Lincoln

Park was now in the poorest tenth of the metropolitan area; just six percent of residents were college graduates. It had also undergone a profound racial transition, as whites left and were replaced by black, Puerto Rican, and Mexican residents. Along the lake, these communities barely had a larger presence than they had in 1950; but west of Larrabee and south of Armitage, they made up a majority of the population.

The rehabbers now addressed this divide with far more realpolitik, and less idealism, than their predecessors twenty years earlier. "The Triangle forms a half-mile buffer strip...protecting a middle class area from a ghetto," the OTTA Planning Committee wrote to the organization's president in an internal memo in 1970. "Without this buffer strip, Lincoln Park as we know it could not exist." The Committee set out OTTA's next task: "The north and east...is now rather stable and the Triangle, to protect its future, must look south and west." In other words, the battle would continue on other fronts.

CONCLUSION

In 1927, Sol Kogan and Edgar Miller bought their rooming house on Carl Street, dreaming of artists in Paris. In 1948, the Old Town Triangle Association formed to update that dream. The rehabbers believed that they had found a special kind of neighborhood where they could build a special kind of community—one that celebrated do-it-yourself creativity and enjoyed middle-class stability while welcoming the kind of people who were shut out of the exclusionary suburbs and cold downtown towers.

The 1970s would, in many ways, mark the end of the dream that Old Town and Lincoln Park could be that Goldilocks neighborhood. It was not that no one wanted that kind of community anymore, but that they looked for it elsewhere. For many in the new generation, Old Town was less a symbol of the hopeful revival of city life than a watchword of what might happen if that revival wasn't handled carefully.

To the north of the Triangle, around the intersection of Broadway and Diversey, young people who had been priced out of Lincoln Park's lakefront districts found a new neighborhood whose virtues they extolled in ways that sounded remarkably familiar. "A multiethnic mix of families, senior citizens, and young people," wrote one resident. On its commercial street, "old women carried straw baskets to their German bakeries, their Jewish meat markets and Greek grocers…. The neighborhood churned in charm and poverty and earthiness." Once just a pocket of the larger Lakeview neighborhood, the young professional arrivals called it New Town.

But almost as soon as it had been rechristened, some of the recently arrived began to complain that New Town was changing for the worse. Ethnic markets were replaced by bars; "creative" shops opened to cater to wealthy tourists from the suburbs. Rents increased. One of these new arrivals, a *Tribune* columnist, had a name for these changes: "Old Town syndrome." Some people were trying to stop it, but for the columnist, it was already too late.

"Those who fled to New Town from Old Town," she wrote, "recognize the corpse."

The people who lived in Old Town would have been surprised to hear that their neighborhood was dead. Measured by property values, middle- and higher-income families, or renovated homes, the community was in better health than ever. Not only that, but these metrics kept moving up—both intensifying where rehabbing had taken hold and spreading into new areas.

Since World War II, Old Town and other nearby parts of Lincoln Park had become hubs for professional class white Chicagoans. In 1950, nine percent of Old Town Triangle residents held a college degree, compared to about six percent for the city as a whole; in 1970, forty-three percent of Old Town Triangle residents held a college degree. For Chicago as a whole, the share had barely budged, reaching just eight percent. The concentration of investment on the North Side extended to both physical housing and college attainment. After 1970, the white professional presence in these areas went from disproportionate to dominant.

Despite frequent predictions that the trend couldn't last—"When the young adults tire of this, they'll move to the suburbs," one skeptic told a reporter in 1969—the share of Old Town Triangle adults with college degrees increased to sixty-two percent in 1980 (versus fourteen percent citywide) and seventy-three percent in 1990 (versus twenty percent citywide). By 2010, it was eighty-six percent (versus thirty-four percent citywide).

The western area of Lincoln Park, where poverty had increased before 1970, reversed course as property values in the east priced out more moderate-income rehabbers. Where Larrabee Street had once stood as a stark dividing line between the rush of investment near the lake and the growing poverty closer to the river, by the 1980s those differences were shrinking rapidly, and by the 2000s they were gone. The most disinvested and stigmatized part of the neighborhood—the southwest corner just blocks from the Cabrini-Green public housing project—saw its college share increase from six percent in 1970 to eighty-eight percent in 2010.

These changes mirrored changes in Lincoln Parkers' incomes. In 1970, median income in Lincoln Park as a whole was still below the citywide average because of the poverty on its western side. Only in 1980—over twenty-five years after the founding of the Lincoln Park Conservation Association, and more than fifty years after Sol Kogen, Edgar Miller, and Jesus Torres began working on their artists' studios—did Lincoln Park's median income surpass the city's. But it kept growing from there, reaching nearly twice the median income in Chicago as a whole in 2016.

Lincoln Park's incipient racial integration fell victim to this growing concentration of wealth. Though in 1950 the neighborhood had been almost entirely white, in 1970, Latino and black Chicagoans made up more than one in five Lincoln Parkers. But the neighborhood's share of Latino or black residents fell by half between 1970 and 2010.

Much of the Puerto Rican community that had existed around Armitage and Halsted had already been displaced by the mid-1970s. Some moved to the Lakeview neighborhood to the north, others west across the Chicago River to Wicker Park and Humboldt Park. The Lincoln Park branch of the Chicago Public Library, which had built a small Spanish-language program in 1970, recommended shutting it down just a few years later because so many of their patrons had left the neighborhood.

Just as rehabbers had spread from outposts like Crilly Court to the rest of Old Town, and then from Old Town to the rest of Lincoln Park, white professionals spread from Lincoln Park to much of the rest of the North Side after 1970. To many, this movement seemed like an antidote to the suburban flight that had stripped wealth from neighborhoods across Chicago. But most of the newcomers replicated the rehabbers' pattern of concentrating their investments in a tight, growing circle, while avoiding the rest of the city. In part as a result, the spread of affluence on the North Side since 1970 has been accompanied by even more widespread growth in disinvestment and poverty in other neighborhoods, especially on the South and West Sides.

As with the early days of rehabbing in the 1940s and 50s—and, indeed, Sol Kogen's decision to buy on Carl Street back in the 1920s—new white collar residents have tended to locate as close to the established zone of affluence as their finances allow, pushing outward towards new areas only once a block is "filled up" with higher-income residents they are unable to outbid for housing. Like the border on Larrabee between the rehabbed Old Town Triangle and the much lower-income areas to the west in the 1960s, the border of gentrification remains sharp even as it moves farther and farther out from Lincoln Park.

The government-financed demolitions and redevelopment that had been so controversial in Old Town and Lincoln Park were, for the most part, absent in places that experienced change thereafter. The urban renewal programs of the 1950s and 60s were essentially shut down by President Richard Nixon in 1973. (Beginning in the 1990s, however, governments began actively reversing their previous investments and demolishing public housing. In neighborhoods near the growing zone of affluence, this often set the stage for an influx of private investment. The Cabrini-Green homes to the south of Lincoln Park are a notable example.)

Private developers have also played a somewhat different role since the 1970s. The rehabbers' continued push to limit the construction of large apartment buildings usually meant fewer, and smaller, changes to the built environment after the 1970s. In 1971, after a four-year campaign by LPCA and others, the Chicago City Council effectively banned four plus ones, the most common kind of new apartments on much of the North Side lakefront. In 1975, the OTTA announced a new initiative to change zoning laws across the Old Town Triangle to reduce densities. The highrise apartment buildings that had been built along Chicago's north lakefront by the scores in the 1950s, 1960s, and 1970s were almost entirely brought to a halt by a wave of zoning laws in the 1970s and 1980s. And in 1977, OTTA won additional protections when the City Council voted to make most of the Triangle an official historic district, preventing demolition of the area's historic housing stock beyond what Project One and Phase Two had already carried out.

"The threat of overdevelopment has replaced the problems of underdevelopment," the OTTA wrote in 1975. "The original objectives of the GNRP included maintaining population at the existing level…. Now we are faced with an increasing over concentration of people."

But Old Town's population was not at the level it had been at the start of the GNRP: It was far lower. In 1950, about 9,700 people had lived in the two Census tracts that covered the Triangle. In 1960, that number had fallen to 8,000, and then 5,500 in 1970, as urban renewal demolitions, private renovations of dense apartments into more spacious homes, and smaller household sizes shrunk the neighborhood. Even after the construction of new homes had filled in the urban renewal redevelopment lots and placed a few additional high-rises along the lake, Old Town had just 6,900 people in 1980, nearly thirty percent fewer than in 1950.

Rather than preventing runaway population *increases*, both the de-densification measures supported by rehabbers' organizations and the changes wrought by private rehabbers and public renewal had served to shrink the neighborhood. Lincoln Park as a whole, which had been home to over 102,000 people in 1950, had barely 67,000 inhabitants in 2016. These declines were driven in part by smaller families, but the loss of housing also played a significant role: Lincoln Park had almost 3,000 fewer homes in 2016 than 1950, a figure that does not include many of the thousands of people for whom home had meant a room in a rooming house.

Without the clear-cutting demolition of Lincoln Park's conservation program, other gentrifying neighborhoods on the North Side did not see such extreme depopulation. But the general rule still held: As communities became wealthier, new residents took up more space than their predecessors, and kept out the kinds of dense housing that might have made up the difference. Lakeview, just north of Lincoln Park, saw its population fall by thirteen percent between 1970 and 2010, even as its median income increased by eighty percent; the population of North Center, west of Lakeview, fell by nineteen percent as its income rose seventy-six percent over the same period. When gentrification jumped to Chicago's Northwest Side, on the other side of the Chicago River, the pattern continued: West Town, including the Bucktown and

Wicker Park areas, lost fifteen percent of its population between 1980 and 2010, as its median income increased by 109 percent.

As these neighborhoods became more sought after than ever before, fewer people were able to live in them, putting pressure on new arrivals to expand the zone of concentrated investment to accommodate more housing over a larger area.

In many ways, the Lincoln Park of 1970—to say nothing of the Lincoln Park of the twenty-first century—did not reflect the diverse, equitable community the rehabbers professed to want in the 1950s. The Battle of Lincoln Park left the neighborhood even further from the kind of community Cha Cha Jiménez, Pat Devine, Rev. James Reed, and their allies and followers fought for. The effects of these failures caused a great amount of harm for the displaced lower-income residents of Lincoln Park, including the constituents of the Poor People's Coalition. Why was this harm not avoided, particularly given the rehabbers' stated goal of preserving the neighborhood's diversity?

One reason is that the scale and power of the forces remaking their neighborhood far exceeded what most Lincoln Parkers understood. Though both the rehabbers and the anti-urban renewal activists pointed to places like Georgetown in Washington, DC or Greenwich Village in New York City—either as exemplars or cautionary tales, depending on their point of view—they could not have known that the movement of middle-class whites back to central cities was a truly national (even international) and durable phenomenon.

By the 1980s and 1990s, researchers showed that what had happened in Lincoln Park was also happening at the same time in many cities around the United States, Canada, and Western Europe. Though local efforts could channel or shape these changes, they were fundamentally driven by larger economic and social forces that LPCA and the Young Lords Organization could not hope to control.

The end of World War Two, for example, unleashed a baby boom that created a sudden surge in housing demand, though very little new housing had been built since the beginning of the Great Depression sixteen years earlier. As rich countries' economies evolved in the decades after the war, service and professional industries grew rapidly, which meant more white-collar workers looking for short commutes to downtown offices. A growing middle-class counterculture movement encouraged some people to think of urban living as an identity statement to distinguish themselves from the suburban mainstream. As young middle-class adults waited longer to marry and have children, the number of people in their twenties or thirties who chose their neighborhoods primarily for access to cultural amenities, rather than schools or yards, increased—and this demographic grew even more as the baby boomers reached young adulthood. Meanwhile, deindustrialization and the environmental movement began to cut down on the urban pollution that had long made city living unpleasant and dangerous.

These forces created remarkably similar paths of change in seemingly very different cities—changes that contemporaries were noting by the late 1960s. As one bemused feature in *National Observer* magazine in 1969 put it: "For a growing number of Americans, happiness is a home in a slum…. The trend is national and unmistakable."

A second reason is that the battles of the 1960s centered almost entirely on the government-funded urban renewal programs of Project One and Phase Two, even though the vast majority of the social changes wrought in the neighborhood were the result of private activity. Lincoln Park's federal conservation program evicted over 2,000 people, a substantial amount by any measure. But the total number of people displaced was many times greater: Between overall population loss of tens of thousands in the decades after 1950 and the rapid demographic shifts and property value increases, one academic estimated in 1979 that 35,000 people had been displaced. Regardless of the exact number, it is clear that the elimination of thousands of homes by individual rehabbers and developers who combined smaller apartments, and the bidding wars that resulted as greater numbers of high-income people sought homes in a shrinking housing market, affected a greater number of households than were directly displaced by government-funded demolition.

At the time, these changes may have been harder to perceive than those imposed by the conservation program. Unlike government renewal authorities, private housing renovators didn't announce a decade's worth of planned changes all at once, or tally up the collective impact of thousands of smaller projects. When private activity did seize the attention of Lincoln Parkers, it was often large individual projects, like the handful of lakefront highrises—but these, too, represented a small fraction of all of the new townhouse renovations, private construction, and rent hikes changing the neighborhood.

Even if Lincoln Parkers had understood the dominant role of private housing market changes, however, it's not clear they would have been able to effectively stop them. Unlike government-funded urban renewal, whose plans could be amended or stopped with the vote of a public body, private renovations were the work of thousands, even tens of thousands, of individuals who were not formally accountable to public pressure. These renovations were, of course, accountable to public laws and regulations about how housing could be added, eliminated, changed, and priced. But using those laws to stop the trend of rising property values would have required the rehabbers (and urban renewal officials) to fundamentally rethink what and who conservation was for.

By the mid-1960s, the rehabbers faced two plausible paths to maintaining an income-diverse neighborhood. They could have tried to halt the rise in property values that was pushing market rents higher than working-class people could afford; and they could have built large amounts of subsidized housing whose rents would not have increased with the market.

But the rehabbers' organizations rejected both of these paths. Philosophically, increasing property values had been a major objective of the movement from the beginning; practically, many rehabbers had sunk massive amounts of money into their home renovations and needed higher property values to recoup their investments. And measures that might have slowed that growth— somehow returning the neighborhood to its pre-1960s status as cut off from major mortgage lending, or allowing the widespread construction of dense new housing to absorb the influx of middle-class residents—were almost unthinkable.

Similarly, rehabbers tended to oppose creating large amounts of subsidized housing. Many worried that such a permanent presence of low-income residents would threaten their property values and drive other middle-class homeowners away. Even after a successful fight to double the number of sites for rent-restricted housing in the late 1960s, Lincoln Park's renewal program offered just sixty family public housing units—a small fraction of the thousands of households that might have qualified for one.

In the end, then, most rehabbers were not inclined to sacrifice other priorities to fulfill their earlier promises of a mixed-income Lincoln Park.

This tangle of powerful national trends and the priorities of those with power to change local policy continued to produce contradictions between the stated desires of rehabbers and the outcomes of neighborhood change. "We were working for a community that had people of all economic levels," one Old Town resident reflected in 1976. "At one time it seemed attainable, now it seems like a will o' the wisp, impossible, naive." Another told an interviewer: "There were certain contradictions in what we wanted. We wanted it to be an integrated neighborhood. And we wanted it to be clean, remodeled, and respectable." (Left unasked was, "Respectable to whom?")

But despite the conclusions of those who saw the Old Town Triangle as a cautionary tale about the incompatibility of rehabbing and economic and racial integration, new rehabbers continued to both search out "diversity" and imagine that their area's future might be different. "I hope that rents will not price out the diversity of the neighborhood," a rehabber in a more central area of Lincoln Park said in 1976. "I don't think that it's so much fun when everybody's the same...you might as well live in the suburbs." But in fact the trajectory of those areas has been similar.

———————

Some people will read the story of Lincoln Park as a kind of salvation, however imperfect. Without the rehabbers, the neighborhood might have followed the path of many other communities around the city: increasing disinvestment, its buildings in worse and worse repair; depopulation as people continued to flee to newer areas; shuttered businesses; vacant buildings and lots; and so on. Many people may look at those options and decide that the displacement of lower-income people in Lincoln Park was an acceptable price to pay to avoid that fate.

But limiting our imaginations to these two choices is a trap. The story of Lincoln Park shows that displacement and disinvestment are not separate processes—they are two sides of the same coin. The deliberate redlining of neighborhoods to cut them off from mortgages or home improvement loans, the poor provision of basic public services, and the racist stigmatization and exploitation of neighborhoods where black or Latino people lived made life increasingly difficult for residents of communities across Chicago. Rehabbers responded by carving out a space where they would be free from those disadvantages. In doing so, they created enormous disparities between "rehabbed" areas and everywhere else in the quality of building maintenance, public services, and the growth of property values.

As a result, new professional class residents who wanted to live in the central city for access to jobs, culture, or community paid handsomely to be on the winning side of this divide. Their willingness and ability to pay more than lower-income residents resulted in displacement, deprived other areas of their resources, and further exacerbated the gap between rehabbed blocks and everywhere else.

If displacement and disinvestment are not opposing choices, but processes that reinforce each other, then they need to be tackled together. Deep inequalities between neighborhoods are both a cause and effect of these processes. A city that ensures that all neighborhoods afford their residents a decent quality of life won't solve all of its problems, but it will deflate the high-stakes bidding wars for housing in high-amenity neighborhoods that drive up prices in some areas and sap resources from others. Such a city may be a "will o' the wisp," but it may also be the only way out of our current trap.

ACKNOWLEDGMENTS

Thanks to everyone who has ever contributed to the incredible treasure that is writing about Chicago and its neighborhoods and people: Arnold Hirsch, Beryl Satter, Brad Hunt, Carla Shedd, Robert Sampson, Eve Ewing, Whet Moser, Natalie Moore, Mary Pattillo, and countless others whose work has been fundamental to so much of my life. Thanks to DePaul University's Special Collections and Archives and the Chicago Public Library archives, without which the bulk of the research that produced this book would have been impossible. Thanks to everyone who read early drafts and gave feedback, without whom this would be an infinitely worse book: Devin Bunten, Amanda Kass, Paul Katz, Nick Kryzcka, Craig Newman, Steven Vance—as well as everyone who attended my Open Newsroom, and Build Coffee for hosting it (as well as for being the place where I finished my final revisions), and City Bureau and particularly Andrea Hart for organizing it. Thanks to Joe Cortright for taking me on at City Observatory and giving me time and guidance to read, talk, think, and write about cities and neighborhoods full time. Thanks to Anne Trubek for asking me to write this book and guiding it when I had no idea what I was doing, and Dan Crissman for doing so much to polish it. Thanks to my parents, Judy and Jason, and my brother, David, for being a wonderful family. Thanks to Beckee for putting up with me while I wrote this. I love you.

SOURCES

A full bibliography is available at battleoflincolnpark.com, but I want to acknowledge some of the people whose own research was most crucial for writing this book.

Materials provided by the Old Town Triangle Association, and particularly Shirley Baugher's books *Our Old Town* and *At Home in Our Old Town* formed a crucial backbone to the narrative.

Lilia Fernández's *Brown in the Windy City* is a go-to source for the history of Latinxs in Chicago, including the Puerto Rican community in Lincoln Park.

Michael Robert Gonzales' 2015 thesis "Ruffians and Revolutionaries: The Development of the Young Lords Organization in Chicago" was key to the final chapters.

Arnold Hirsch's *Making the Second Ghetto* is foundational for anyone writing about midcentury urban renewal in Chicago.

José Cha Cha Jiménez and the archival work done at the "Young Lords in Lincoln Park" collection hosted at Grand Valley State University greatly informed the later parts of the book.

David Ley's The *New Middle Class and the Remaking of the Central City* provided important national and international context.

A. Rod Paolini's 1970 thesis "Lincoln Park Conservation Association: The Politics of a Community Association" was enormously helpful.

Margaret Stockton Warner's 1979 dissertation "The Renovation of Lincoln Park: An Ecological Study of Neighborhood Change" was completely invaluable.

Harvey Zorbaugh's *The Gold Coast and the Slum* contains a wildly entertaining and detailed description of Tower Town and the Gold Coast.